THE GOSPEL OF LOVE

A Meta-Translation

Ὁ Θεὸς ἀγάπη ἐστίν

Meta-Translation, Introduction, and Notes by Mark Arey
Original Translation and Appendices
by Mark Arey & Philemon Sevastiades

Dark Bird Publishing
Taos, NM

Published in 2017 by Dark Bird Publishing
925 Paseo del Pueblo Sur, Taos, NM 87571

ISBN: 0-9981065-1-8
ISBN-13: 978-0-9981065-1-9

THE GOSPEL OF LOVE

A Meta-Translation

Table of Contents

THE GOSPEL OF LOVE

A Meta-Translation

Introduction

If a flower had a God, it would not be a transcendental flower but a field – moreover a field as described in physics, an integrated pattern of energy, a field which would not only be flowering, but also earthing, raining, shining, birding, worming, and beeing. A sensitive flower would, through its roots and membranes, feel out this entire pattern and so discover itself as a particular exultation of the whole field.

Alan Watts[1]

---

[1] Alan Watts, *In My Own Way: An Autobiography* (New World Library, 2007), pg. 182.

What if what we thought about God proved not to be God, but only our concepts about God? What if the God of Abraham, Isaac, and Jacob had never been squared with the philosophy of Socrates, Plato, and Aristotle? What if the Apostles had turned East instead of West? And what if God was not a Being at all, but rather the ground of all being? What if?

For the past ten years, I have been wrestling with how best to live as a Christian in this last portion of my earthly life. Since I was a Greek Orthodox priest for over thirty years, it seemed that I should have had it sorted out by now. However, looking back through the decades, I see now just how uncomfortable I was in my priestly skin. From my earliest childhood memories, I trace in my consciousness an unmistakable line demarcating God as always outside, a transcendent Supreme Being, an Ultimate Reality beyond any conception or conceiving, an Other I could never reach.

I was raised to believe that Jesus was the way into the life divine, and I went on a lifelong quest to know him.[2] But as thirteenth century Sufi poet Rumi wrote:

> "I have lived on the lip of insanity, wanting to know
> reasons, knocking on a door. It opens.
> I've been knocking from the inside."[3]

---

[2] Malachi Martin's *Jesus Now* is a good guide to the landscape of this search (Dutton, 1973).
[3] Translation by Coleman Barks, *The Essential Rumi* (Harper One, 2004), pg. 281.

Yes, I had been knocking from the inside all along, unaware that's where Jesus had been knocking as well.[4] I invited him into my heart as a teenager, as counseled by those who seemed to know best. I worshipped with Charismatics and Pentecostals, sought with earnest Evangelicals, explored with Roman Catholics, and argued with Mormons and Jehovah's Witnesses. All the while, I was a committed Episcopalian.

Then in my college years, inspired in part by the writings of the Roman Catholic monastic Thomas Merton and in part by my love of classical languages, I found my way to Orthodox Christianity. And although it was an egoistic aspiration on my part, I was determined to become a priest. In seminary, I read voraciously, dialogued incessantly, and poured my mind into containers made by others. Knocking from the inside all the while.

Orthodox Christianity, with its luxuriant liturgical life and rich aesthetic, can be a marvelous religious experience. But those externals are designed to be portals to a deeper reality. I arrived at this magnificent threshold thinking it to be the inner sanctum of absolute truth. And the more I studied, the farther I felt from Jesus, the one who for our sakes subjected himself to hatred, alienation, and death, and in turn was subjected to centuries of speculation about his nature.[5]

Nevertheless, the decades of my active ministry as a priest proved to hold many gifts. The greatest of these was the extraordinary privilege to be with fellow human beings in their

---

[4] Cf. Revelation 3:20.

[5] Those studying Divinity (another way of saying, Theology) encounter this vast sea of turbulence in the Christology portions of their dogmatics classes.

suffering, their pain, and their dying. In these encounters, I experienced the wondrous transformational power of love. I witnessed with my own eyes – as an *autoptes*[6] – how knowing that one is loved and giving oneself to love can transfigure the most unthinkable ordeal into a revelation of peace, reconciliation, and happiness. Beholding these miracles of love, I will always hold the priesthood in unending gratitude and honor, even though I left that vocation some years ago for the sake of a different kind of love. What is more, I bear an everlasting debt to all those who allowed me to share in their grace-filled exits, which were the best lessons in theology I ever learned. But for all the grace – even grace upon grace – witnessing such suffering is also a profoundly troubling challenge.

You see, serving an omnipotent God is a double-edged sword. The first cut: If God is omnipotent, then the Divine Being clearly doesn't need any help to do anything. Why would any ministry be necessary in the first place? The second cut is deeper still: If God is truly omnipotent, why is there so much wrong and evil in this world? The intellectual pursuit of this question is known as theodicy, the branch of theology which seeks to answer that intractable question of ancient Greek philosophy: "Whence evil?"[7] God certainly has had public defenders through the ages who line up their arguments to justify the Divine dignity, but such

---

[6] Cf. Luke 1:2, "eyewitness."

[7] Greek, πόθεν τὸ κακόν.

arguments pose a further question: Why does an almighty God need defending in the first place?[8]

These are very hard questions with no easy answers. For church institutions and faith communities, such questions shake the very foundation stones of their self-definition. They put religious bodies on the defensive and usually the faithful are just told to "have faith," as if belief were a commodity like rice or gold. Rather than opening up people to freedom, I have found that institutional religion – once challenged in any way – tends to become even more autocratic and more domineering. It morphs into a means of control for those perpetuating, or in some cases perpetrating, a belief system. At its best, spiritual practice flowers into transformation of person, community, and reality itself. At its worst, in the case of full-blown absolutists – those who hold their creed to be the one and only truth – we have all witnessed the destructive capabilities of any religion that becomes weaponized by hatred and violence. As Karen Armstrong has so pointedly observed:

> "When something inherently finite – an image, an ideology, or a polity – is invested with ultimate value, its devotees feel obliged to eliminate any rival claimant, because there can be only one absolute."[9]

---

[8] David Bentley Hart's, *The Doors of the Sea: Where was God in the Tsunami?* is a densely written example of such a defense (Wm. B. Eerdmans Publishing Co., 2011). C. G. Jung's *Answer to Job* is a fascinating alternative view, (trans. R. F. C. Hull, in *Psychology and Religion*, v.11, Collected Works of C. G. Jung, Princeton University Press, 1973).

[9] Karen Armstrong, *The Case for God* (Alfred A Knopf, 2009), pg. 38.

As difficult as it may be for us to recognize, this sense of absolute correctness about our beliefs does not come from any religion's founder, basis, or text. We cannot lay such blame on any individual's claim, no matter how lofty. Absolutism initiates within our own minds. We have to take responsibility for it and come to terms with it. The fact is that we enter this world in complete relativity, dependent on everyone and everything for sheer existence, and we are trapped in misknowledge[10] about reality. We falsely believe that we are inherently real – separate and absolute on our own – because we *feel* ourselves to be so. Thomas Merton put it this way:

> "Modern man, in so far as he is still Cartesian (he is of course going far beyond Descartes in many respects), is a subject for whom his own self-awareness as a thinking, observing, measuring and estimating 'self' is absolutely primary. It is for him the one indubitable 'reality,' and all truth starts here. The more he is able to develop his consciousness as a subject over against objects, the more he can understand things in their relations to him and one another, the more he can manipulate these objects for his own interests, but also, at the same time, the more he tends to isolate himself in his own subjective prison, to become a detached

---

[10] "Not merely a failure to know something, which we mean by ignorance, but a knowing something wrongly, a thinking we know rightly when we mis-know." *The Life and Teachings of Tsongkhapa*, edited by Robert A. F. Thurman (Library of Tibetan Works and Archives, 2006), pg. 282.

observer cut off from everything else in a kind of impenetrable alienated and transparent bubble which contains all reality in the form of purely subjective experience. Modern consciousness then tends to create this solipsistic bubble of awareness – an ego-self imprisoned in its own consciousness, isolated and out of touch with other such selves in so far as they are all 'things' rather than persons."[11]

Moreover, projecting this absolute sense of "I," "Me," and "Mine" on to an imagined deity, we end up creating an absolute God in our own image. Quite the reverse of the account in Genesis, in which a plural Deity creates us in 'their image, according to their likeness.'[12]

Thus it was after thirty years of ministry, I commenced a search in hitherto unexplored regions of my heart and mind for a new way forward. I reengaged my imagination, positioned myself to be astonished, and waited to be amazed. To my unending delight, two wonderful things happened.

First, I re-discovered a long forgotten gift from my late friend and priestly colleague, Father Philemon D. Sevastiades. (This meta-translation is the fruit of our labors together nearly twenty years ago.) Philemon's gift to me was a reintroduction to Buddhism through the person and work of Professor Robert A. F. Thurman, a leading scholar of Tibetan Buddhist thought in the Western Hemisphere. Philemon had studied with Thurman as an

---

[11] Thomas Merton, *Zen and the Birds of Appetite* (New Directions, 1968), pg. 22.
[12] Genesis 1:26.

undergraduate at Columbia University and generously shared with me his deep appreciation for Thurman's brilliance. I had read in Buddhism as a young man, but only briefly. Looking back in the rear-view mirror of experience, I see now how unsettled I was by the Buddhist non-theistic worldview. Afraid to venture out of my comfort zone, I settled for an unthinking commitment to the religion I was raised with, a Christianity I inherited from others.

Second, years after Philemon's untimely death in 2004, I met the love of my life, my wife Lyn, a woman of profound spiritual depth. She opened my heart to reality and re-presented to me the Buddhist tradition. Living in New York City, we became members of Tibet House US (the Dalai Lama's cultural center in America), which was founded in 1987 by none other than Professor Thurman himself. With reinvigorated interest and eager curiosity, I began to attend lectures, read books and articles, and, most significantly for me as a translator, read translations of Buddhist texts.[13]

Studying the Buddhist point of view was immensely gratifying, and it made me feel more, rather than less, Christian. After years of dull, dormant repetition, I felt like my faith was growing again, like I was waking from a long sleep. The Buddhist tradition of knowledge and understanding not only elucidated

---

[13] I sought Professor Thurman out and vividly remember introducing myself to him at an evening event at the 92nd Street Y in New York City, where he shared the stage with the early Christian scholar Elaine Pagels, a remarkable academic with whom I heartily disagree on certain points (see Appendix II). To this day, I hold dear a copy of Thurman's *Why the Dalai Lama Matters* that he signed for me that evening.

deeper meanings of the Gospel, but also helped me to transform faith into experience.

I suspect that most people would not think that Buddhism and Christianity have very much in common. Some Christians are surprised to learn that the ethical teachings of each tradition are strikingly similar. But what is more significant is that they both possess the same understanding of the nature of reality. Discovering this mutual awareness, viewing my Christian faith through a new lens, has been deeply inspiring to me, a gift I want to share with others. Hence this book.

The two basic doctrines of Christianity, the Trinity of Persons of the Godhead and the Incarnation of the Second Person in Jesus, teach a view of reality that is scarcely mentioned in Churches today. Even if these doctrines are, in one way or another, shared among all Christians. What follows is my attempt to share a new perspective of understanding these teachings through a Buddhist lens, freshly expressed in a meta-translation of the Gospel of John. I hope this perspective will help the reader discover or even re-discover a treasure of the Christian Gospel buried too long in accretions of human making.

* * *

The meta-translation itself is adapted from a translation of the Gospel of John on which Philemon and I had collaborated, and which his premature death prevented us from completing. In preparing the meta-translation, I have continued to refine and edit the original work, as the process of translation is never truly finished, merely settled on at a particular moment in time.

Philemon and I had the grand design to translate the entirety of the New Testament from the official Greek text of the Orthodox Christian Church into modern, accessible English. We commenced our enterprise in the year 1999 by working backwards through the New Testament. In 2003, with the help of great friends John and Anne Mavroudis, we published our first translation, *Apocalypse: The Book of Revelation*, in our own imprint.[14] We worked from the official text that was published by the Ecumenical Patriarchate of Constantinople in 1904.[15] In keeping with the tradition of nomenclature that gives us *Textus Receptus* (the Received Text that is the basis for the King James Version), and *Textus Criticus* (the Critical Text that is the basis for the Revised Standard Version and most modern translations), we christened it *Textus Constantinopolitanus*. This Greek version, as I wrote in my translator's note for *Apocalypse*:

> "...is the living text of a living, praying, worshipping Church. It is based on the ancient ecclesiastical tradition of the Great Church of Christ of Constantinople that embodies the continuous memory of the Orthodox Christian Church."[16]

Apocalypse was intended to be the first of many volumes; sadly, it was the end of our project. When Philemon died unexpectedly on August 27, 2004, our work together died with

---

[14] Mark Arey and Philemon Sevastiades, *Apocalypse: The Book of Revelation* (Oracle Publishing Group, 2003).

[15] *E Kaine Diatheke engrisei tes Megales tou Christou Ekklesias*, *The New Testament sanctioned by the Great Church of Christ* (Constantinople, 1904); sometimes referred to as the "Antoniades" edition.

[16] Arey and Sevastiades, *op. cit.*, pg. xxxii.

him. I note, with great admiration and a longing for more, Philemon's brilliant introduction to *Apocalypse*.[17] It is a masterfully composed theological and liturgical exposition on the Book of Revelation that should be read by anyone seeking to understand this most enigmatic Christian text.

After Philemon's passing, the remainder of our work was left to gather dust as I moved on to a full-time parish assignment. Years passed, but I never gave up the hope that our translations would one day reach the light of day. I have long desired to put our unpublished material into the public sphere. This has proven to be challenging, and I have grappled with how to do so. When the chance came to re-release *Apocalypse* in an unexpected format, I embraced the unusual opportunity.[18]

Philemon and I had agreed that he would write the introduction to our translation of the Gospel of John, which was regrettably left unfulfilled. I am grateful and humbled to now present our translation of the Gospel of John as a meta-translation, *The Gospel of Love*, and the introduction has fallen to me. In putting our work into the public eye, I do so with abiding gratitude for Philemon's life and legacy. He is not here to say whether he is

---

[17] Arey and Sevastiades, *op. cit.*, pp. xi – xxvi.

[18] *Apocalypse* was re-published in a graphic novel format in 2012 by Zondervan as *The Book of Revelation*. The full translation was published, brilliantly adapted by Matt Dorff and spectacularly illustrated by Chris Koelle. Many thanks are due James Webb III and Dr. Vaughan Allen for their support of this publication. Dorff and I collaborated again with draft material of the canonical Four Gospels that Philemon and I had worked on, which I polished and arranged into a *Diatessaron*, a narrative harmony based on all four canonical Gospels. The volume covered the life of Jesus from his birth right up to the moment before his baptism. It was also published by Zondervan in 2013 as the graphic novel, *Messiah: Origin*, expertly adapted again by Dorff and beautifully illustrated by Kai Carpenter.

pleased with the result, but the truth is that I came to the decision to undertake this endeavor inspired by a dream in which he dramatically appeared. The details of the dream have evaporated from memory, but its resonance remains powerful. When I awoke, I was convinced that it was by meta-translation that our work was to find its audience.

I have included and amplified the footnotes from the original work, as well as its two Appendices. Appendix I is the very last thing Philemon and I ever worked on. I distinctly recall our excited conversations as we labored toward our conclusion. Appendix II was very dear to Philemon's heart, as the relationship between Jews and Christians was of keen interest to him, and he worked passionately for interfaith understanding. As I reflect now on Appendix II and our insistence on translating text within context, I see the first hints of my own movement beyond polysemic translation[19] to meta-translation.

Philemon was the most intelligent priest I have ever known: sharp, bright, and above all committed to the power of words. "Words count," he would say to me, and I owe him a great debt for the wisdom and inspiration he imbued in me. Translating and writing with him was an exceptional pleasure and honor for which I shall forever be grateful.

* * *

---

[19] Polysemic translation allows for more than one analogue to register the meaning of a word, and takes into account the context of the word. Many literalists prefer the monosemic approach and insist on only one meaning, regardless of the context. This, I believe, accounts for much of the repetitive and often dull character of some biblical and even liturgical translations.

So, what exactly is a meta-translation and how does it work? At first even the expression, meta-translation, might seem redundant, as "*meta*" is the Greek for the "trans" in "translation." Indeed, the word translation, *metaphrasis* in Greek, literally means "to carry speech [from one language into another]." But meta-translation should not feel so unfamiliar. We are used to hearing about meta-narrative, meta-data, and even meta-comedy. But the question remains: Beyond conveying the meaning of the words in a different tongue, what more is being offered?

The answer starts with the purpose of every translation, which is an invitation to the reader to hear and see the text anew with fresh ears and fresh insights. A translation succeeds because the melody of words, grammar, syntax, etc. that it creates corresponds to that of the original piece, much like playing a symphonic piece on a single instrument. Though clearly not the same, the notes are discernible and the melody recognizable.

Meta-translation goes further. It invites the reader to hear the notes played on a new and indeed strange instrument, like playing Bach on a didgeridoo. This creates a very different experience, changing words in order to realize meaning. Meta-translation strives to plumb the very roots of the text's essence, its *mythos*. As a teacher of mine once told me, "A myth is a lie that tells a deeper truth." This just might be the most concise way to describe meta-translation, for as the saying goes, "all translators are liars." Meta-translation broadens context and widens parameters of meaning in order to express the ultimate significance of a text. At the same time, it seeks to undo certain prejudices of language that are inevitable consequences of culture. The shifts in vocabulary may be slight. The effect? Anything but.

In *The Gospel of Love*, the meta-translation imaginatively expands the horizon of meaning by changing three specific words. These words are teeming with enormous power: God, Father, and Lord. When Jesus, John the Baptist, John the Evangelist (in his capacity as narrator), or one of Jesus' disciples/followers uses any of them (Lord, in specific instances only, see below), they are meta-translated by the single word, Love.

This holds true as well when these actors quote from the Old Testament. There are however, three exceptions in the case of Jesus: 8:54, where he is enlightening the Pharisees; 10:34, where the plural, gods, is left as is; and 16:2, where the context seems to require it to remain as is. In four cases where God and Father are closely paired (5:18, 6:27, 8:42, 20:17), Father is meta-translated with Begetter in the first two instances, with Parent in the third, and left as Father in the last, in order to avoid close-quarter repetition.

As mentioned above, Lord, *Kyrios*, is a special case. Only when it is clearly being used by one of the aforementioned as an appellation for God (*Adonai* in Hebrew) is it meta-translated as Love. When Jesus' followers address him as Lord, they are not referring to him as *Adonai*, but as their own lord and master, so there is no meta-translation in these cases.

As for Jesus' other interlocutors, the words God and father are left as is (except in the case of 8:19 to retain the sense of irony, a literary device the Evangelist employs throughout). *Kyrios* is translated as the context dictates: Lord (*Adonai*), lord, mister, or sir.

Another expansion of context in the meta-translation is the treatment of the words *amartia* (sin), *sozo* (save), *krino* (judge), and *mathetes* (disciple). Given the importance of these words, it seems prudent to qualify their treatment in advance.

Amartia literally means failure to hit the mark. The alpha privative (*a/martia*) signifies that something is askew, apart from where it should be.[20] *Amartia* does not have a moral emphasis in and of itself. Its root meaning is somewhere between an error in judgment and a mistake. It can be translated as sin, but this word is loaded – some would say overloaded – with intimations of shame, self-loathing, and degradation. *Amartia* can just as easily be translated as error, failing, fault, and even guilt – any of which signals quite a different tonality. The meta-translation employs each of the above, as well as sin, in order to broaden our understanding of human shortcoming.

The verb *sozo* does have the meaning to save from something, or to deliver out of harm's way, but it also can mean to heal. Choosing to translate it as heal is a way of inviting the reader to identify the whole ministry and sacrifice of Jesus as something beyond a narrowly defined legalistic and substitutionary death that somehow appeased Divine wrath and saved the human race from eternal damnation. Our salvation is much more than heading to heaven rather than hell. It is a process of healing, of becoming

---

[20] The parallel from Buddhism is the concept of suffering, the first of the Four Noble Truths. The word suffering is *dukkha* (Pali), which literally means a wheel that is misaligned and does not revolve properly.

whole human persons and engaging with others in healing and indeed salvific ways.

Krino (judge – the noun *krisis*, judgment) is also a crucial word for consideration, as judging others is something all of us too often do, contrary to Jesus' teaching.[21] Like the word sin, judge and judgment are laden with moralizing and emotional accents that narrowly constrict the meaning of Jesus' message. *Krino* can just as easily mean to decide, or to choose; both of which are used in the meta-translation. Judgment is overrated and pales in comparison to mercy and compassion. Those who preach the hell-fire damnation of others are more often than not the very ones mired in their own failings and projecting them onto everyone else. The seventh century Christian mystic, Isaac of Syria, has this to say of such:

> "Mercy and justice in one soul is like a man who worships God and the idols in one house. Mercy is opposed to justice. ... As grass and fire cannot co-exist in one place, so justice and mercy cannot abide in one soul."[22]

The noun *mathetes* has special challenges because of the current cultural overlay that the word disciple implies, to wit, the unwavering adherence of a devotee. In the original Greek, *mathetes* has the basic meaning of student or pupil. In the Jewish world of the first century of the Common Era, those who followed particular rabbis were called their students, or disciples. The word,

---

[21] Matthew 7:1.
[22] Homily 51, *The Ascetical Homilies of Saint Isaac of Syria* (Holy Transfiguration Monastery, 2011), pg. 379.

disciple (from the Latin *discipulus*), has an original meaning of a learner, pupil, scholar, even an apprentice. The word takes on special meanings in the Gospels, depending upon usage. Chiefly, *mathetes* references the Twelve Disciples, who are also called apostles (those who are sent).[23] Jesus called his disciples with the invitation "Follow me" (Hebrew, *lech aharai*, "walk after me"[24]), which was the common call of the itinerant teacher (rabbi) of the Torah.[25] *Mathetes* can also refer to one of the Seventy Disciples (Luke 10:1-24), as well as any and all of the followers of Jesus.

Restricting the meaning of *mathetes* merely to an adherent can lead to an unnecessary and unfortunate diminishing of the learning process to which Jesus calls us. Learning to love our enemies not only in word but in deed, to forgive from our hearts those that wrong us, and to show mercy and compassion to the stranger; these are not accomplished on the day we decide to follow Jesus. They are lifelong educational pursuits. Too often, Christians give up or ignore this demanding vision of discipleship in favor of a discipleship of doctrinal and/or personality-driven positions that are filtered through agendas not Jesus' own. In the meta-translation that follows, *mathetes* will be translated with

---

[23] See the lists in Matthew 10:2-4, Mark 3:13-19, and Luke 6:12-16.

[24] See the expression in 6:66, where disillusioned and confused by Jesus' teaching on his flesh and blood as food and drink, many of his followers "no longer walked after him," (Greek, *ouketi met' autou periepatoun*).

[25] John the Evangelist comments (1:38) that "rabbi translated means teacher." In Jesus' day it was a term of respect for a teacher, literally meaning "my master." The Evangelist Luke employs a unique word for Jesus, *epistates*, usually rendered as "Master" (literally, "one who stands over") and reserves the word *didaskalos* (teacher), for any other rabbi, including John the Baptist.

alternates in order to remind the reader that following Jesus is as much an educational calling as it is a conviction of personal belief.

Meta-translation also requires a few more adjustments, which follow of necessity for the purposes of a more natural flow. The possessive pronoun "my" is usually omitted where the original reads "my Father" in Jesus' dialogues. Another major shift occurs where personal pronouns are required. Linguistically, Love (*agape*) is a feminine word in Greek. Consequently, feminine pronouns are utilized where needed. This might disturb some readers who may see this as a gender polemic. It is not. I fully understand that there are readers for whom the weight of male-dominated speech and language in Christian history feels natural. I believe a case can be made for a corrective usage, seeing that in Christ there is neither male nor female.[26] More to the point, it seemed to me that committing to the radical notion of meta-translation in the first place required an accompanying 'radical' pronoun.

For references to the Holy Spirit, it has been traditional to translate the neuter pronoun of the original with masculine pronouns, even though in Greek, "spirit" (*pneuma*) is neuter. Spirit in Hebrew (*ruach*) is feminine and many Christian thinkers have seen in the Spirit the feminine complement to God. Be that as it may, for the purposes of the meta-translation, the neuter pronoun will be employed.

Additionally, one of the principles of this work as translation is not to prejudice the reader/hearer by automatically

---

[26] Galatians 3:28.

translating every male pronoun in the teaching of Jesus as "he" or "him," unless the referent is a specific male person. When both men and women are being referenced in Greek, as in all Indo-European languages, it is in the masculine plural, a linguistic habit inherited from Sanskrit. Where gender specificity can be avoided without damaging the integrity of the meaning, it is, by employing the second person plural in English as an alternative to the third person singular of the original Greek. This has the advantage of simultaneously universalizing and personalizing the material across time and culture.

Jesus spoke not only for the first century audience in his presence. His *logos*, his message, was spoken for all time. Consider the following three translations of John 11:9,10, beginning with the King James Version:

> *11:9) Jesus answered, "Are there not twelve hours in the day? If any man walk in the day, he stumbleth not, because he seeth the light of this world. 11:10) But if a man walk in the night, he stumbleth, because there is no light in him."*

In the Revised Standard Version, "any man" becomes "any one," but the maleness of the verse remains, even though it is clearly directed to everyone, male and female alike.

> *11:9) Jesus answered, "Are there not twelve hours in the day? If any one walks in the day, he does not stumble, because he sees the light of this world. 11:10) But if any one walks in the night, he stumbles, because the light is not in him."*

The meta-translation takes the "any" one step further. By employing the second person plural rather than the third person singular, the integrity of Jesus' discourse is left intact and extended to all readers/hearers.

> *11:9) "Are there not twelve hours of daylight?"*
> *Jesus answered. "If any of you walk in the daylight,*
> *you will not stumble, because you behold the light*
> *of this world. 11:10) But if you walk in the darkness*
> *of night, you will stumble because the light is not in*
> *you."*

Finally, as part of dilating the Passion narrative, portions of that narrative as told in the Gospels of Matthew, Mark, and Luke have been inserted into the Johannine narrative flow. These passages include all that Jesus is recorded as speaking from the Cross, as well as some details from his crucifixion not in the Johannine account. Such an arrangement of verses derives from the ancient tradition of the *Diatessaron*, a harmony of the Gospels mentioned above. This *sermo* of Jesus – delivered from the pulpit of the Cross – his last words as Son of Man, seemed indispensable for a more complete understanding of his crucifixion.[27] The additional verses will be placed into the order of the Johannine text with an asterisk marking the beginning of each insertion, and ending with a footnote identifying their source.

---

[27] For Christians, Jesus destroys death by death, an understanding mirrored in the Buddhist tradition by Yamantaka, the wrathful form of Manjushri, who is the bodhisattva personification of wisdom. This parallel is further investigated in the forthcoming companion volume, *The Kingdom of Love: Living on Earth as it is in Heaven.*

I fully expect that these shifts and adjustments will make some readers uncomfortable. For others, they may be downright intolerable and smack of heresy. Yet for others, I hope they may provide a welcome sense of relief. Whatever one's reaction to the sounds and symbols, I would ask the reader not to rush to judgment until giving the text an opportunity to unfold. Like an ancient scroll, one cannot see the end in the beginning. Likewise, you will not hear the message of this meta-translation unless you allow yourself to listen to the full implication of this *logos*, which is more discourse than pronouncement, as much a flowing river (*sermo*) as a single drop (*verbum*).[28]

For those who absolutize Scriptural verses and believe that life is in them,[29] this meta-translation is likely in vain. But for those more firmly committed to the meaning of the text, I hope that what follows will swell their imaginations and amplify their realizations about God in a deeper and perhaps new way. This may sound like a rather abstruse attempt of allaying fears that I am meddling with the Christian Gospel. That is hardly the case. Rather, I propose this meta-translation of the Gospel of John, *The Gospel of Love*, as an invitation to a deeper understanding and lived faith. My hope is that this is an unveiling – an apocalypse, if you will – of the profound truth to which the Gospel calls us.

* * *

---

[28] For those interested in how early Christian thinkers considered the meaning of *o Logos tou Theou*, see "Reopening the Conversation on translating JN 1,1" by Marjorie O'Rourke Boyle; found in *Vigiliae Christianae*, Vol. 31, No. 3 (Sep., 1977), pp. 161 – 168.

[29] Cf. 5:39.

Christianity was born in the desert. It was a faith come forth from the Jewish people, a faith whose Scripture was the Torah and the Prophets. But hundreds of years before the birth of the Jesus, the desert God had already collided with the Greek world that Alexander the Great left in the wake of his conquests. The monotheism of the Old Testament served a deep yearning in the Hellenic mind. In the Jewish God, Greek Christians discovered an answer, a supreme governing principle. They found a solution to the age-old problem of "the One and the Many" by identifying the "One" with God and the "Many" with creation. But as the pillar of fire of Moses became ensconced in the pillars of the stoas of Athens, the problem re-emerged. How to reconcile the one God of the Old Testament as the three distinct persons of the New? How could one be three and three one? And as for Jesus: how could he be both God and human? Easy questions to pose, but how much ink and blood have been spilt trying to answer them!

For Christians, the first five centuries of the Common Era were virtually obsessed with creating a framework where the one God of the whirlwind of Job could be understood as Father, Son, and Holy Spirit. The minds of these early Christians acknowledged something that was nowhere explicit in Sacred Scripture[30]   a

---

[30] The one so-called exception is the famous *Comma Johanneum* (I John 5:7,8), absent from nearly all ancient Greek manuscripts, but included in the Textus Constantinopolitanus (as well as Textus Receptus). It reads: *7) For there are three who bear witness in heaven: the Father, the Word, and the Holy Spirit, and these three are one. 8) And there are three that bear witness on earth: the Spirit, the water, and the blood, and these three are one.* Most biblical scholars agree that it is not the original text, which reads in most Greek manuscripts: *7) For there are three who bear witness: 8) the Spirit, the water, and the blood, and these three are one.* In the prefatory matter to the 1904 *E Kaine Diatheke*

Trinity of Divine Persons who were, nevertheless, one God. From the simple declarations of the Nicene Creed (standard for most Christians), to the intricate and subtle investigations of the Cappadocian Fathers[31] and Augustine of Hippo, thinkers of these early Christian centuries struggled to express the Divine in a way that was consistent with the message of Jesus, yet within an intellectual framework comprehensible to the Hellenic world.

As for Jesus, over the centuries he has been dissected to the point that his "Godmanhood" has become as stripped of meaning as a cadaver is empty of blood.[32] Jesus' self-emptying, his *kenosis*, is relegated to theories about his relation to the Godhead, rather than understood as the quintessence of relational activity that leads to the kingdom of God.

If we look at the course of Christian theology, the God of Jesus was ultimately identified with the God of the philosophers – the Supreme Being or Unmoved Mover – and Jesus himself was literally incorporated into the Godhead. He was not only Son of God, but God Himself, a Divine Person of the Holy Trinity. He had been worshipped by his followers in the Gospel (9:38), and this could not have been righteous, from the monotheistic point of view, unless he were God. The climax of the Gospel of John (20:28) is often seen as this reveal.

(*op. cit.*), after stating that the *Comma* is upheld neither in the manuscript sources nor the patristic tradition, its inclusion is explained thus: "It is preserved in accordance with the opinion of the Holy Synod."

[31] Basil the Great, Gregory Nazianzen, and Gregory of Nyssa.

[32] For an exhaustive survey, see *The Oxford Handbook of Christology* (Oxford University Press, 2015).

Similarly, Jesus' mission became principally identified with the sacrificial offering of himself for the life of the world. For some strains of Christianity, this has meant a tremendous infusion of stigma into the consciousness of every believer from the moment of baptism. The stress is on our failings, our sins. Obligation, duty, and service are the rule; judgment, shame, and guilt the tools of enforcement. The Church then morphs from a loving and supportive community to bailiff, judge, and jury, and unfortunately in too many cases throughout history, executioner.[33]

These historical developments have much more to do with human beings and their self-appointed interpretations of the message of Jesus, than with the message itself. Whether you read this meta-translation or any other translation, it is clear that Jesus is engaged in something far beyond a set-up for a subsequent institutional guilt trip. For all the talk of the "blood of the Lamb," did he not end animal sacrifice when he cleansed the Temple?[34] For all the talk of the coming "Judgment Day," did he not refuse to judge anyone?[35] Indeed, he who was guiltless and without sin stood silent before an unjust judge who dared to sit in judgment![36] Moreover, if you read carefully, you will see that his constant and consistent provocations of the Pharisees and religious authorities, both in word and deed, are much more than rabbinical back and

---

[33] Not content with declaring the translator John Wycliffe a heretic nearly thirty years after his death, the Church exhumed his remains thirteen years later in 1428, burned them, and threw the ashes in a river. This, for the man who gave us the first translation of the New Testament in the English language.

[34] 2:13-17.

[35] 8:1-11,15; 12:47.

[36] 19:13

forth. They are consciousness-raising exercises, "dharma" talks,[37] if you will, for unenlightened beings.[38]

* * *

For most Christians, the Trinity and the Incarnation of the Second Person in Jesus are vague concepts of God and definitions severely limited by language. These conceptual notions have become wrapped in liturgical/symbolic intimations and imitations of the transcendent. Valuable in and of themselves, especially when they serve as a liminal introduction to the transcendent, they are nonetheless not experiences of the immanent, "like clear water or blue sky."

The doctrine of the Holy Trinity is like some secret, absurd mathematical formula: $1+1+1=1$.[39] The first of the Ten Commandments: "Hear, O Israel: the Lord our God is One Lord"[40] hangs over every Christian thinker like a sword of Damocles, waiting to fall on the suspicion of any denial of monotheism. "Trinity" has been reduced to a formulaic expression at which we must hurriedly cross ourselves and think of a triangle, three interlocking circles, or an old man, a lamb, and a dove. The central doctrine of Christianity has become irrelevant to our spiritual quest, rather than the core activity it is intended to be, a purposeful

---

[37] Dharma is the "doctrine of the Buddha; it has the two aspects of instruction and understanding, the former being what one learns and the latter, one's internal realization." Geshe Wangyal, *The Door of Liberation* (Wisdom Publications, 1995), pg. 227.

[38] E.g., 7:23; 8:6-8; 9:39-41; 10:34-38.

[39] When I was a boy, growing up in the Episcopal Church, I was taught that understanding the Holy Trinity was like looking at a bowl of fruit from three different angles. Even at ten years old, I found the explanation lacking, and I still wondered about all the other angles.

[40] Deuteronomy 6:4.

way of living that mirrors the activity of the Trinity, a ceaseless flow of love. [41]

Jesus has seen the same kind of spiritual arithmetic: 1+1=1. Debates raged for centuries as to *how* he is Son of God, both divine and human. The God-Man to some, a good man to others, and everything else in between. Christian communities have come and gone like the grass of the field, debating, fighting, and even warring over which version of Jesus was the 'real' Jesus. In the meantime, Jesus' radical and dynamic vision of unconditional love for all creation goes unheeded and even unnoticed.

Trinity and Incarnation: doctrines that speak of multiplicity and unity, of diversity and oneness. The centrality of unity for Christianity encompasses the oneness of God, the oneness of Jesus, and the oneness of the Church.[42] Christians have found diverse (and sometimes perverse) ways to express this through the centuries, without realizing that the "one thing needful"[43] has been with us all along.

It is through our very differences, and the way we use them to exceed our limits as individuals, that we overcome our self-centeredness and achieve unity. Through our connectedness to one another, we realize not only the truth of Christianity, but the truth of reality itself. The apostle Paul put it this way:

---

[41] "Trinity was an activity rather than an abstract philosophical doctrine. It is probably because most Western Christians have not been instructed in this exercise that the Trinity remains pointless, incomprehensible, and even absurd." Karen Armstrong, *op. cit.*, pg. 117.

[42] Cf. Ephesians 4:4-6.

[43] Luke 10:42.

"For, just as the body is one but has many members – yet all the members are of one body even though they are many in number – the body is one. This is how Christ is also. We were all baptized by one Spirit into one Body, whether we are Jews or Greeks, slaves or free. And we all drank of one Spirit. And so, the Body is not one member, but many. If the foot should say, 'I am not a hand; I am not of the body,' is it then something else than of the body? Or if the ear should say, 'I am not an eye; I am not of the body,' is it then something else than of the body? If the whole body were an eye, how would we hear? Or if the whole body were an ear, how would we smell? But as things truly are, God has set the members in the body – each one of them – as he has willed. But if everything was just one member, where would the body be? As it is, the members may be many, but the body is one. How can the eye say to the hand, 'I don't need you!' Or again, how can the head say to the feet, 'I don't need you!' Rather, those members of the body that seem to be weaker are much more necessary. Likewise, those members of the Body which we deem less worthy of honor, on them we bestow all the more honor. And our members that seem unbecoming have even more comeliness, but those that are comely have no need. Nevertheless, God has configured the Body, granting more honor to the one that lacks, so that there might be no division, no schism in the Body, but that members might have the same care and concern for one another. So, if one member suffers, all the members empathize; and if one member is praised, all the members rejoice. Now you are the Body of Christ and each member, a part."[44]

This paradigm of the Church has been given to every generation of Christians, who have had, each in their turn, the opportunity to realize this model of unity for the last two thousand years. But our history speaks for itself. Differences have spawned violence, persecution, and hatred that manifest even to this day. Yet we *are* called to take the Message of the Gospel seriously, not selectively. The insistence of Jesus on this unity must be taken at least as seriously. How passionately he speaks of this oneness in the penetrating seventeenth chapter of the Fourth Gospel:

"… that they may be one, even as you, Father, are in me and I am in you, that they may also be one in us, that the world might believe that you sent me. And the glory that you gave to me, I have given to them, that they might be one, even as we are one; I in them and you in me, that they might be perfected in one, so that the world might know that you have

---

[44] I Corinthians 12:12-27, translation my own, with "Body" capitalized to indicate the Church.

sent me, and that you love them even as you love me."[45]

Is it possible to find our way above the fray of all the multiplicities of doctrine, dogma, and divisiveness of local churches, communities, and traditions? The answer is nearer and simpler than we think.

The answer is love.

* * *

Love: pure, clear, compassionate, merciful, unalloyed love. For God *is* love, ὁ Θεὸς ἀγάπη ἐστίν.[46] And if God is love, then love is also God, not some Supreme Other Being, a philosopher's Unmoved Mover, dwelling beyond the created order. Nor an Olympian or Desert Deity with a fickle personality, ready to destroy one day and redeem the next.

For Christians, love is the benchmark against which all theological speculation must be measured. If those preaching and teaching God are not speaking in terms of love, then the God of whom they speak is a false god, an idol.[47] Their preaching and teaching are projections of their own minds, mere notions and concepts about a God who does not even exist, an idol of their own making. And unlike physical idols of stone, metal, and wood, such conceptualizations are more insidious:

"Verbal definitions of God in the form of creeds, dogmas, and doctrines are far more dangerous idols than statues made of wood, stone, or gold, because

---

[45] 17:21-23.
[46] I John 4:8
[47] Cf. I John 5:21.

they have the deceptive appearance of being more 'spiritual,' and because a creedally formulated God has been reduced to words, and is no longer experienced immediately, like clear water or blue sky."[48]

God is infinite, without any boundary or event horizon. There is no thing and no place that God does not saturate. God is love, and love is God. Love overcomes all duality and opposition. Love goes beyond subject and object. Love brings all multiplicities into unity. Love is the underlying and ultimate reality of the universe. Love is the unified theory of everything.

The implications of this should be staggering. In the spiritual life, anything done apart from love is anything but spiritual. I realize that there are many for whom rules make all the difference; the rules and regulations set the boundaries that some of us seem to need in order to function. But who was ever born with a list of "dos and don'ts" in their heart?

Do we really need some outer force to inform us that murder, thievery, and lying disfigure our humanity? Perhaps as a species we needed such guidelines in the distant past, and maybe some of us still do. But think about it; who is born filled with hate? Children famously do not differentiate, much less reject, other human beings on the basis of appearance, color, ethnicity, sexuality, or affiliations, be they political or religious. We learn to hate. We are taught to fear. We are trained to resent. Such lessons mire us in a dangerous and destructive misknowledge of our true

---

[48] Alan Watts, *op. cit.*, pg. 76.

nature. These are the "sins of the fathers," that Scripture speaks of.[49]

The fact is that we are born with complete vulnerability and in desperate need – need for love, care, compassion, and mercy – and all at the hands of others. We are unable to feed ourselves, clean ourselves, to warm or comfort ourselves. We are born in utter dependency, something that for the most part we biologically overcome as we grow into adults. But we never lose our need for connection to others. Our relationality persists. We may repress it, suppress it, or both, but it is always there, the ground and root of our human nature. We need to love and to be loved. It is our essential human nature, because it is the nature of everything.

At one time or another, all of us have experienced love: a mother's love, a father's love, a grandparent's or a relative's love, a spouse's love, a lover's love, a friend's love, a pet's love. Even if our current ability to appreciate such love is diminished or even damaged beyond ostensible repair, even if we have no accessible memory of love, we have all known something of love at one point or another during the course of our lives. What is more, within our deepest selves, we yearn for love and we need to love. Without love, the world loses meaning and even the grandest palace becomes a dim and dreary prison. But with love, even the darkest prison shines brighter than any Versailles or Alcázar.

* * *

In my reading and study of Buddhism, what Christians call God/love, Buddhists call bliss/emptiness (or voidness). How

---

[49] Cf. Exodus 34:7.

Buddhists describe the nature of reality struck me from the very first as a parallel of the Christian view. As I noted above, the faith of Jesus traveled West, not East: to the intellectual descendants of Socrates, Plato and Aristotle; not to Nagarjuna, Aryadeva and Asanga.[50] For two millennia, Christianity has been encased in the Western philosophical tradition, with all its benefits and hindrances. I believe that it is time to refresh the optics of Christian theology by looking through new lenses. This does not mean that two thousand years of intellection about Jesus should be abandoned; rather, it means that we should fearlessly pursue what our liberation in Christ truly means. I hold this meta-translation as only a beginning word, which I hope will be a creative impetus in Christian thought.

Buddhism has remained, by and large, substantially beyond the borders of Christendom, with the Zen tradition being perhaps the most familiar, if often misunderstood, in the West. But as a result of the invasion, genocide, devastation, and unjust occupation of Tibet by the Communist Chinese governments over the last seventy years, the Buddha Dharma has traveled not only from East to West but around the world, carried by the longsuffering exiled Tibetan people led by a simple monk, the much-beloved and extraordinary Fourteenth Dalai Lama. I have been the beneficiary of this Dharma through hearing teachers of integrity and reading texts transmitted from Buddhist 'rabbis' of both past and present.

---

[50] Nagarjuna (2nd c. CE), Aryadeva (3rd c. CE) and Asanga (4th c. CE) are three of the Seventeen Pandits (scholars) of Nalanda Monastery, the most famous Buddhist institution of India (5th – 13th century CE).

That is why this meta-translation could just as easily have been named a *metta*-translation, for the homonym *"metta"* (Pali, or *maitri* in Sanskrit) means love – powerful compassionate lovingkindness. In the Buddhist tradition, *metta* is expressed as a profound love for all beings, described with intensity in the *Karaniya Metta Sutta* as follows:

> "Even as a mother protects with her very life her child – her only child, so with a limitless heart should one love all living beings."[51]

The Christian and Buddhist paths both affirm the experience of love as going beyond oneself for the sake of the other. To give oneself through love beyond the duality of feeling absolute and distinct, beyond the "I" and the "Thou" of self and other. To love fully and completely is the realization of the oneness of everything, to melt into the infinite nature of all, because love is all and all is love. Yet, the experience of melting into the infinite is with full and conscious compassion toward all beings, with the realization that you are all beings, and all beings are you. Though the body has many members, it is one body. We are all connected. This is the realization of the truth of Love, the ultimate reality.[52] This is the true Passover, the passing over from death to life.

In the Buddhist tradition, ultimate reality is called bliss or emptiness (or voidness). Emptiness (Sanskrit, *sunyata*) does not mean nothingness, or blankness, much less anything nihilistic. This emptiness is not a state or condition; rather it is the realization that

---

[51] *Sutta Nipata*, 1.8.
[52] Cf. I Corinthians 13:13.

nothing is an absolute in and of itself. It is the awareness that all things are relational, all things are interdependent.

The great Buddhist philosopher, Nagarjuna (c. 150 – 250 CE), gives a concise and dense definition that articulates emptiness as the reality of relativity. With simple and yet profound eloquence, he states:

> "Whatever is relativity, we proclaim that emptiness. It is dependent designation. It is also the central way. Nothing whatsoever is found which is *not* relativistically originated. Therefore, nothing whatsoever is found which is not empty. So if all things were *not* empty, there would be no origination and no destruction."[53]

His Holiness the Dalai Lama puts it another way:

> "Reality may be one, in its deepest essence, but Buddha also stated that all propositions about reality are only contingent. Reality is devoid of any intrinsic identity that can be captured by any one single proposition – that is what Buddha meant by 'voidness'."[54]

Therefore, in Buddhism, as in physics, there is no thing that is absolute. Everything is relative. Everything is dependent on relationality and is made of bliss/love. And if we truly believe that God is love, then everything is not made by some distant Supreme

---

[53] Quoted in *The Central Philosophy of Tibet: A Study and Translation of Jey Tsong Khapa's Essence of True Eloquence*, by Robert A. F. Thurman (Princeton University Press), 1984, pg. 158 (emphasis in original).
[54] H.H. Dalai Lama, interview in *Mother Jones*, Nov/Dec 1997.

Being dwelling somewhere apart in a heaven of our imaginings. Everything is made *of* love and we are all configurations of love. Everything is made *of* God and we are all configurations of God.[55] When our experience is that of missing the mark (sin) and suffering, we could be called disfigurations of bliss/love, but we are bliss/love nonetheless. When we miss the mark, when we suffer, we are unfulfilled love, unrealized bliss. Then is our awareness limited to the cycle of change and suffering, of origination and destruction, which is called *Samsara*[56] in the Buddhist tradition, and *Kosmos*[57] in the Christian.

In Buddhist language, liberation from that cycle of change and suffering, birth and death, is called *Nirvana*,[58] and those who realize it are "enlightened" or Buddha. They have become fully aware, fully conscious, fully awake, knowing that nothing is absolute, that everything is relative. They have realized voidness. From a Christian point of view, they are risen from the dead and have awakened to their true nature.[59] They are living "on earth as it is in heaven," actualizing the only prayer that Jesus ever taught us.[60] They love through complete self-emptying.

Unfortunately, Christians have been conditioned to believe that everything is absolute, made by an absolute God. In Christian theology, this is based in part on a philosophical doctrine, *creatio*

---

[55] Cf. 10:34.

[56] Literally, "wandering through" in Sanskrit.

[57] Greek, "world." Note that Jesus does not wish to take his disciples out of the world, only preserve them from its evil (17:15)

[58] Literally, "extinguished" or "blown out" in Sanskrit.

[59] Cf. Ephesians 5:14.

[60] Matthew 6:9-13.

ex nihilo, a teaching not found in Sacred Scripture and adopted by Christian philosophy hundreds of years after Jesus.[61] It posits God as absolutely uncreated and everything else as absolutely created by God. It creates a gulf between the Creator God and the creation, absolutizing both, separating both. Christians are taught that this gulf between the uncreated God and the created world is bridged in Jesus, for "through him all things came to be, and apart from him, nothing that exists came to be."[62]

However, where Creator ends and where creation begins remains a blur. The separation of an absolute Creator from an absolute creation is an unsatisfying tenet of faith that relies more on a suspension of experience than an experience of knowing. [63] Grasping at our own sense of being, we feel absolute. Apprehending ourselves as fixed and permanent, we cut ourselves off from our relational capacities. Others become objects of our desires and vehicles of our machinations. We fail at loving and

---

[61] Karen Armstrong (*op. cit.* pg. 372) defines *creatio ex nihilo* as "the phrase used to distinguish the new doctrine of creation that emerged in the Christian world during the fourth century and stated that God had created the world out of absolute nothingness. This cosmology had been unknown in the ancient world."
[62] 1:3.
[63] In the Orthodox Christian Church, the distinction in the Godhead of "essence" and "energies" was articulated as a way to understand how the transcendent (essence) could be immanent (energies). This theological position is often referred to as "Palamite," for Saint Gregory Palamas, the 14th century theologian and bishop of Thessaloniki who defended monastic prayer practices called hesychasm; see John Meyendorff, *A Study of Gregory Palamas* (St. Vladimir's Seminary Press, 2010). For Orthodox Christianity, this distinction purports to preserve the duality of the uncreated God and the created order. I see it another way, as a Christian approach to circumscribe the unified ultimate reality with language: Essence/Energies, Absolute/Relative, One/Many, Heaven/*Kosmos*, *Nirvana*/*Samsara*.

overcompensate for the abjectness we feel deep inside. Out of this grasping insecurity within, we project our imagined absoluteness into the universe like a movie on a screen, filling the space of our lives with our own vanity. We create an absolute God in our own image, replete with our passions, cravings and impotencies. How else could an Almighty Creator so totally fail at the stewardship of creation, unless it was as we have failed at it ourselves?

* * *

There is another way of understanding God, through the doctrines of Trinity and Incarnation, one that is steeped in the theological tradition of Christianity. The Trinity is chiefly about the *relationship* between the Divine Persons, about their relativity, about their activity, that one cannot be without the other. In Greek, this is called *perichoresis*, "inter-dwelling." The eighth century theologian John of Damascus follows a long line of theologians using this word to describe the inner life of the Holy Trinity:

> "The ground and the abiding of the [Divine] Persons is in each other; for they are undivided, inseparable from one another, *inter-dwelling* one another without loss of identity."[64]

This same understanding of reality exists in the Buddhist tradition. The Vietnamese monk Thic Nhat Hanh has coined the word "interbeing" (verb "inter-be") to describe this same relativity:

---

[64] John of Damascus, *De Fide Orthodoxa Libri Quattor*, J.P. Migne, *Patrologia Graeca*, Paris 1857-66, 94.860B (translation my own).

"To be is to inter-be. You cannot just *be* by yourself alone. You have to inter-be with every other thing."[65]

This total and complete relativity, one within the other(s), is, at the same time, total integrity. It is through relativity, through emptiness (Greek, *kenosis,* Sanskrit, *sunyata*), that the life of the Trinity is lived. The Father is only the Father as he *empties* himself into the Son and the Spirit. The Son is only the Son as he *empties* himself into the Father and the Spirit. The Spirit is only the Spirit as it *empties* itself into the Father and the Son. One cannot be without the other. Each completely transcends their own being, utterly inter-being, or inter-dwelling, in the other.

If you compare the two – *kenosis* from the Christian tradition and *sunyata* from the Buddhist – what stands out at once is that the emptiness that describes the life of the Holy Trinity in the former describes the nature of reality in the latter. But if the nature of reality is love, is God, then *kenosis*, emptiness, *is* the basis of everything.

This same emptiness, this same *kenosis*, is precisely what Jesus taught us by his life, his message, his sacrificial death, and his bodily resurrection. The Apostle Paul describes it in his letter to the Philippians:

> "Truly, let this mindset be in you, which was in Christ
> Jesus, who, existing in the form of God,
> did not regard being equal to God as something to be

---

[65] *The Heart of Understanding: Commentaries on the Prajnaparamita Heart Sutra* (Parallax Press, 2009), pg. 3, (emphasis in original).

grasped, rather, *he emptied himself,*

taking the form of a slave

born in the likeness of humankind.

Being found in human configuration,

he humbled himself,

became obedient unto death,

even death by the cross.

Therefore, God has exalted him

and granted him a name that is above every name,

that at the name of Jesus

every knee shall bow – of those in heaven,

on the earth and under the earth,

and every tongue shall confess

that Jesus Christ is Lord,

to the glory of God the Father."[66]

In becoming flesh by his incarnation – a supreme self-emptying – Jesus imparted to the world of his day, and to the world for all time, a living portrait of the reality of love. Jesus was, as the hymn says, a "human configuration"[67] of love. As such, his life was a continuous witness to the transformative power of love; a power so strong that it could heal body, mind, and soul. Even conquer death.

We are called to live by this same self-emptying, to shine with the same light in which Jesus was transfigured on Mount

---

[66] Philippians 2:5-11, my own translation. Most scholars believe these verses to be a hymn.

[67] Philippians 2:8 (Greek, καὶ σχήματι εὑρεθεὶς ὡς ἄνθρωπος).

Tabor.[68] The fourth century theologian Athanasius of Alexandria summed up all Christian theology and the ultimate meaning and purpose of Jesus' incarnation for us in a single sentence:

"For he became a human being, so that we might become god."[69]

Imagine that! We are all called to become divine, to become love, to become what we indeed already are. This is our highest calling and our deepest reality. And such a life is not beyond our reach. The very form of our humanity teaches us that we are utterly relational, designed to inter-dwell, to inter-be.

Consider our bodies. From a survival point of view, we are physically one of the most vulnerable species. We are not naturally clothed in armor, but in soft skin. We don't have claws that maim, but hands that touch. We don't have fangs that maul, but mouths that speak. We reproduce by an act of love, and mothers first feed infants from their own bodies. Everything about our human form manifests that our natural state is relational, as configurations of love.

If we were aware of this – if we were awake to this – we would know our nature is love and our calling is to be instantiations of love – God enfleshed in *our* humanity – just as Jesus was. Like Jesus, we would love all beings – not just human beings but all sentient beings – even as a mother loves her only child.[70] Like Jesus, we would extend compassion, mercy, and

---

[68] Cf. Matthew 17:1-9, Mark 9:2-10, Luke 9:28-36.

[69] *De Incarnatione Verbi* 54, J. P. Migne, *Patrologia Graeca*, Paris 1857-66, 25.192B (Greek, Αὐτὸς γὰρ ἐνηνθρώπισεν, ἵνα ἡμεῖς θεοποιηθῶμεν).

[70] Jesus describes his ultimate sacrifice of love on the Cross as a mother giving

forgiveness in every instance,[71] not just those convenient to our understanding and to our liking. We would sacrifice our very lives for the benefit of other beings, counting ourselves blessed to do whatever was necessary for the happiness and blissfulness of others.

As Jesus said in his own immortal words:

"This is my commandment: love one another as I have loved you. You can have no greater love than this, to sacrifice your life for your friends."[72]

That is what this meta-translation is all about, presenting the Message of the Word in a way that empowers every Christian believer to live beyond mere words and engage the ultimate reality of love. It is a call to take seriously the words of the Word and embrace the fullness of the Gospel. It is an invitation to go beyond the mundane dictates of religious conformity and to embrace the true love that can change the world. It may seem a long way off, across a turbulent and vast ocean of suffering – lives lived misaligned and missing the mark – but it has been accomplished by enlightened beings through the ages, and it is still being done today.

I am grateful to have lived long enough to catch even the faintest glimpse of that distant longed-for shore. Like the disciples'

---

birth (16:21). Many early Christian homilists describe the Cross as a bed where Christ birthed a new humanity from his side that was pierced after he willingly succumbed to death, even as Adam 'birthed' Eve from his side after he was put into a deep sleep in the garden (Genesis 2:21-24).

[71] Luke 23:34.

[72] 15:12,13 (Greek, Αὕτη ἐστὶν ἡ ἐντολὴ ἡ ἐμή, ἵνα ἀγαπᾶτε ἀλλήλους καθὼς ἠγάπησα ὑμᾶς. Μείζονα ταύτης ἀγάπην οὐδεὶς ἔχει, ἵνα τις τὴν ψυχὴν αὐτοῦ θῇ ὑπὲρ τῶν φίλων αὐτοῦ).

struggle to cross the Sea of Galilee in the storm, the journey of life is often thwarted by winds that swell without warning or apparent reason. Even so, the Lord Jesus comes to us to still the storm of fear inside our hearts, and to awaken us to how very close we always were to that seemingly distant harbor.[73] I am also deeply grateful to the Three Jewels[74] for their radiance in undiscovered regions of my mind, a lamp unto my feet and a light unto my path.[75] "Therefore it is said, 'Awake, O sleeper, and rise up from the dead, and Christ shall shine on you!'"[76]

In sharing this, my heart's truth, my wish is that you receive it and awaken to your own true nature, which is love. Empty yourself of what you think is your self. Trust in your faith. Hold on to your hope. But remember, the greatest of these is love.

---

[73] 6:21.

[74] "These three main aspects of Buddhism, the Buddha, the Dharma, and the Sangha – Teacher, Teaching, and Community – came to be known as the Three Jewels (Skt. *Triratna*) of Buddhism, that is, the three most precious things for the individual seeking liberation from ignorance and suffering." *The Tibetan Book of the Dead*, translated by Robert A. F. Thurman, Quality Paperback Book Club, 1998, pg. 15.

[75] Psalm 119:5.

[76] Ephesians 5:14.

THE GOSPEL OF LOVE

A Meta-Translation

ὁ Θεὸς ἀγάπη ἐστίν

Chapter 1

1:1) In the beginning was the Logos – the Word. And the Word was present to Love; indeed, the Word was Love. 1:2) He was in the beginning, present to Love. 1:3) Through him all things came to be, and apart from him, nothing that exists came to be. 1:4) In him was life, and his life was the light of humanity. 1:5) And the light shines on in the darkness, never overcome by the darkness.

1:6) There was a man was sent from Love whose name was John. 1:7) He came to witness to the light, so that all might believe through him. 1:8) He was not the light, only the witness to the light.

1:9) The true light was the Word, who enlightens every person coming into the world. 1:10) He was in the world, and the world came into existence through him, yet the world knew him not. 1:11) He came to his own, yet his own received him not. 1:12) But as many as did receive him, who believed in his name, on them he bestowed authority to become the children of Love, 1:13) begotten not by blood, nor by lust of the flesh, nor by human desire, but by Love.

1:14) And the Word enfleshed, a human tabernacle dwelling among us. And we beheld his glory, the glory of the Only-Begotten of Love, overflowing with grace and truth.

1:15) John bore witness of him, crying aloud and saying, "This is the one of whom I spoke, 'He who comes after me is before me, for he was before me'!"

1:16) All of us have partaken of his fullness, and in grace upon grace. 1:17) The Law was given through Moses; grace and truth are through Jesus Christ. 1:18) No one has ever seen Love. HE WHO IS[77] in the bosom of Love, the Only-Begotten Son, has made Love known.

1:19) This was the witness of John, when the religious authorities[78] sent priests and Levites from Jerusalem to ask him, "Who are you?"

1:20) His declaration was public, withholding nothing. "I am not the Christ!"

1:21) "Then who?" they demanded of him. "Are you Elias?"

---

[77] This capitalization is used to translate the Greek of the Divine Name "Ο ΩΝ" (the LXX translation of the Tetragrammaton, "YHWH"), revealed to Moses at the Burning Bush (Exodus 3:14, LXX), often translated, "I AM WHO I AM."
[78] Greek, *Ioudaios*, see Appendix II.

"No, I am not," he replied.

"Are you the Prophet?"[79]

"No," John answered.

1:22) "So who are you?" they insisted.

"We must give an answer to those who sent us!"

"What do you say about yourself?" [80]

1:23) "I am the voice of one crying in the wilderness," John exclaimed, "'Make straight the way of Love!' as the Prophet Isaiah proclaimed." [81]

1:24) Those sent by the Pharisees 1:25) demanded of him, "If you are not the Christ...."

"Not Elias...."

"Not the Prophet...."

"Then why do you baptize?"

1:26) "I baptize with water," John answered, "but there is one standing among you whom you do not know. 1:27) He is the one who comes after me, who was before me, the strap of whose sandal I am not worthy to loosen." 1:28) All this took place in

---

[79] Deuteronomy, 18:15.

[80] These and similar verses are translated so as to differentiate voices, rather than the unrealistic picture of a chorus of voices speaking in unison.

[81] Isaiah 40:3 (adapted).

Bethany,[82] beyond the far shore of the Jordan River, where John was baptizing.

1:29) The following day, John saw Jesus coming toward him and cried out, "Behold! The lamb of Love, who cleanses the error of the world! 1:30) This is the one of whom I said, 'The man who comes after me is before me, because he was before me.' 1:31) Yet, I did not recognize him! Still, this was the reason I came baptizing with water, so that he would be revealed to Israel. 1:32) I saw the Spirit descending like a dove from the sky, abiding upon him," John continued his testimony. 1:33) "Still, I did not know him! But the one who sent me to baptize with water said to me, 'If ever you see the Spirit descend upon someone and abide with him, that is the one who baptizes with the Holy Spirit.' 1:34) And I did see and I did testify that this man is the Son of Love!"

1:35) The next day, John was standing in the same place again, and two of his students were with him. 1:36) As Jesus walked by, John looked squarely at him and said, "Behold, the lamb of Love." 1:37) The two students heard John's utterance and followed Jesus.

---

[82] Other ancient manuscripts call this place, "Betharaba" or "Bethabara." It is traditionally placed on the east bank of the Jordan and is not to be confused with the Bethany that was home to Lazaros, Martha, and Mary.

1:38) Jesus turned around and saw them following him. "What are you looking for?" he asked them.

"Rabbi," they replied, "where are you staying?" ("Rabbi" translated means "Teacher.")

1:39) "Come and see," Jesus answered them. So they went and saw where Jesus lodged and remained with him the rest of the day. This happened at the tenth hour.[83]

1:40) Andrew, the brother of Simon Peter, one of the two who had heard what John said, followed Jesus. 1:41) But first he went and found his brother, the aforementioned Simon.

"We have found the Messiah!" Andrew announced to him. (Messiah is "Christ" – the "Anointed" in translation). 1:42) And Andrew led Simon to Jesus.

When he saw Simon face-to-face, Jesus exclaimed, "You are Simon, the son of Jonas; you shall be called Cephas!" (which translates "Peter" – the "Stone"). 1:43) The next day, Jesus decided to go to Galilee and finding Philip, enjoined him, "Follow me!" 1:44) (Philip was from Bethsaïda,[84] the same town as Andrew and Peter.)

---

[83] Four o'clock p.m.
[84] A town on the eastern shore of the Sea of Galilee.

1:45) Philip then went and found Nathaniel, declaring to him, "The one Moses wrote about in the Law and the Prophets! We found him! Jesus, the son of Joseph, from Nazareth!"

1:46) Nathaniel quipped to Philip, "Can *anything* good come from Nazareth?"

Philip answered, "Come and see!"

1:47) Jesus saw Nathaniel approaching and remarked about him, "Look! A genuine Israelite in whom there is no guile."

1:48) "How do you know me?" Nathaniel queried him.

"Before Philip called you," Jesus answered him, "I saw you under the fig tree."

1:49) "Rabbi!" Nathaniel blurted out, "you are the Son of Love! You are the King of Israel!"

1:50) "Because I told you, 'I saw you under the fig tree,' you believe?" Jesus countered. "You will see greater than this." 1:51) Then Jesus said to him, "Amen, amen, I say to you! From this moment on, you will behold the sky opening wide, and the angels of Love ascend and descend upon the Son of Man!"

Chapter 2

2:1) Three days later, there was a wedding in Cana of Galilee, and the Mother[85] of Jesus was there. 2:2) Jesus and his students were also invited to the wedding.

2:3) When the wine ran dry, the Mother of Jesus said to him, "They have no wine."

2:4) Jesus replied to her, "My Lady, what concern is that to us?[86] My hour has not yet come."

2:5) His Mother said to the servants, "Whatever he tells you to do, do it."

2:6) There were six stone amphorae[87] in the vicinity, arranged in accordance with Jewish purification rituals. Each held

---

[85] In the Greek text of this Gospel, the Virgin Mary is referred to only as the "Mother" of Jesus. The appellation will be capitalized throughout.

[86] The expression, *Ti emoi kai soi, Gunai*? has often been problematic for translators. Two points should be made. First, the use of *Gunai* (vocative case of "Woman") is not a term of disrespect but of respect, as well as a term of endearment; see entry in Liddell and Scott, *A Greek-English Lexicon* (Clarendon Press, 1996), pg. 363, I. Second, the expression *Ti emoi kai soi* (literally, "what to you and to me") is used by an interlocutor to question the supposed joint interest of the interlocutor and another party in a given matter. As such, the construction is considered an ethical dative, "often used to denote the interest of the speaker, or to secure the interest of the person spoken to;" Herbert Weir Smyth, *Greek Grammar* (Harvard University Press, 1984), pg. 343, par. 1486. It is used in the Septuagint seven times, with some plural forms. It appears in the New Testament only two other times, in two versions of the Gergesene demoniac's questioning of Jesus (Mark 5:7, Luke 8:28). The expression is neutral, and to impute more would suggest that Jesus interrogated his mother in the same way a demon interrogated him. An unlikely scenario.

[87] Greek, *hydria*, large vessels for water.

9

between two and three bath.[88] 2:7) Jesus bid the servants, "Fill the amphorae with water." And they filled them up to the brim. 2:8) Then he commanded them, "Now ladle some out and present it to the banquet master." And the servants presented it.

2:9) But when the banquet master tasted the water now become wine (unaware of where the wine had come from, though the servants who had drawn the water knew), he called out to the bridegroom, 2:10) "Everyone serves the good wine first, and when all are flush with drink, then the poorer stuff, but you have saved the good wine for last!"

2:11) Jesus performed this, the beginning of his signs, in Cana of Galilee in order to manifest his glory, and his students began to put their faith in him.

2:12) Later on Jesus, his Mother, his brothers and sisters,[89] and his students went down to Capernaum and stayed there for a

---

[88] The Greek word is *metretos*, signifying the Hebrew word *bath*, a unit of liquid measurement of about 10 gallons.

[89] The Greek, *adelphoi*, can refer to both male and female siblings (see Introduction, page xxiv). Mark 6:3 mentions his brothers: Iakovos, Joses, Simon, and Judah, and specifically references his "sisters" (*adelphai*), without naming them. According to the tradition of Orthodox Christianity, all are children of Joseph by a previous marriage and the two sisters are Mary and Salome. Salome is identified as the wife of Zebedee and the mother of Iakovos (James) and John the Evangelist. Other traditions hold all these seven persons to be Jesus' cousins, rather than step-brethren; still others believe them to be subsequent children of Joseph and the Virgin Mary.

10

few days.[90] 2:13) Then, as the Jewish Passover[91] was approaching, Jesus went up to Jerusalem.

2:14) In the Temple, Jesus encountered those who sold cattle, sheep, and doves, as well as the moneychangers[92] in their stalls. 2:15) He took some pieces of rope and fashioned a small whip. He drove them out of the Temple, including the sheep and the cattle. Then, Jesus spilled over the pennies of those who exchange the money of the poorest folk[93] and overturned their tables.

2:16) "Get them out of here!" he shouted at those who sold the doves.[94] "Do not turn the House of Love into a house of traffickers!" 2:17) (His followers were later to remember that it is written, "Zeal for your House has consumed me."[95])

2:18) Some of the Judeans[96] confronted Jesus. "What sign can you show us that allows you to do this?"

---

[90] Capernaum was a town on the western shore of the Sea of Galilee.

[91] The first of three Passovers in this Gospel.

[92] All Gentile coinage with graven images was required to be converted into shekels for use in the Temple.

[93] The Greek word *kollybistes* indicates a special kind of moneychanger who dealt in the smallest denominations.

[94] The dove (pigeon) was the offering usually made by the poorest folk, including his own parents (see Luke 2:24).

[95] Psalm 69:9.

[96] Greek, *Ioudaios*.

2:19) "Destroy this temple," Jesus replied, "and in three days I will raise it up."

2:20) "It took forty-six years to build this Temple!" they[97] objected.

"And you are going to raise it up in three days?"

2:21) But Jesus was speaking of the temple of his body. 2:22) Therefore, when he was risen from the dead, his followers remembered that he had said this, and they believed in the Scripture and in the Message that Jesus preached.

2:23) While Jesus was in Jerusalem for the Passover feast, many people came to trust in his name, because they saw the signs that he performed. 2:24) For his part, Jesus did not entrust himself to them, for he knew them all. 2:25) Indeed, he needed no proof about humankind, for he already knew what was inside the human person.

---

[97] *Ibid.*

Chapter 3

3:1) One of the Pharisees, a leader of the Judeans, a man named Nikodemos, 3:2) came to Jesus by night. "Rabbi," he said, "we know that you are a teacher come from God. Truly, no one could do the signs that you do unless God were with him."

3:3) "Amen, amen, I say to you," Jesus responded to him, "unless you are born anew, from above, you cannot see the kingdom of Love."

3:4) "How can someone – an old man no less – be born?" Nikodemos queried him. "Is it possible to re-enter your mother's womb and be born a second time?"

3:5) "Amen, amen, I say to you," Jesus answered, "unless you are born of water and of spirit, you cannot enter the kingdom of Love. 3:6) What is born of the flesh is flesh, and what is born of the spirit is spirit. 3:7) Do not be surprised that I told you: You must be born anew. 3:8) The wind[98] blows where it wills and you hear its sound, but you do not know whence it comes or where it goes. So it is with every person who is born of the wind."

3:9) "How is this possible?" Nikodemos asked him.

---

[98] Greek, *pneuma*, normally translated "spirit." Here translated "wind" (and so at the conclusion of the verse), to show the vibrancy of the metaphor.

3:10) Jesus replied to him "You are a teacher of Israel and you do not know these things? 3:11) Amen, amen, I say to you, we know of what we speak. We testify to what we have seen, and yet none of you receive our witness. 3:12) If you do not believe when I speak of the terrestrial, how will you believe when I speak of the celestial? 3:13) No one has ascended to heaven – except he who descended from heaven – the Son of Man, who is in heaven. 3:14) Indeed, as Moses exalted the serpent in the wilderness, so must the Son of Man be exalted, 3:15) so that whoever believes in him might not perish, but lay hold of life eternal. [99]

3:16) "Truly, Love so utterly loved the world, giving the Only-Begotten Son so that everyone who believes in him might not perish, but possess eternal life. 3:17) Truly, Love sent the Son into the world not to judge the world, but so that through him, the world might be healed. 3:18) Those who believe in the Son are not judged. But those who do not believe have already chosen, because they did not trust in the name of the Only-Begotten Son of Love.

3:19) "And the proof is this, light came into the world, but people loved the darkness more than the light, because their deeds

---

[99] Numbers 21:4-9

were wicked. 3:20) Truly, all those of hateful deeds hate the light. They dare not approach the light, for fear that their actions will be exposed. 3:21) But those who act from truth come to the light, so that their deeds will be revealed as being sustained by Love."

3:22) Afterwards, Jesus took his students into the Judean countryside and passed the days with them there, performing baptisms. 3:23) John, too, continued to baptize in Aenon near Saleim,[100] because there was a great deal of water there. People kept coming to be baptized. 3:24) (John had not yet been cast into prison.) 3:25) A discussion arose between some of John's pupils and a certain Judean concerning rituals of purification.

3:26) John's students went to him and said, "Rabbi, the one who was with you on the other side of the Jordan…"

"To whom you bore witness…"

"Look! He is baptizing…"

"And everyone is going to him!"

3:27) John reassured them, "No person can receive anything, unless heaven grants it. 3:28) You are my witnesses; I said, 'I am not the Christ, but I am sent before him.' 3:29) The one

---

[100] Near the border of Samaria, west of the Jordan River.

with the bride is the bridegroom. The bridegroom's friend, who stands by his side and listens to him, rejoices with special delight at the bridegroom's voice. So this, my joy, is now complete. 3:30) He must increase and I must decrease."

3:31)[101] The one from above is above all things! But the one of earth is earthly and speaks of earthly things. 3:32) The one from heaven is above all things! Indeed, the one from heaven bears witness to what he has seen and heard, yet no one accepts his witness. 3:33) Those who receive his witness confirm that Love is true. 3:34) Truly, the one whom Love sent speaks the words of Love, for not by measure does Love bestow the spirit. 3:35) Love cherishes the Son and has entrusted everything into his hands. 3:36) Those who believe in the Son gain life eternal, but those who do not believe in the Son will not see life; rather, the furor of Love will remain upon them.

---

[101] There are some translations (e.g., KJV, NASB) that continue the voice of John the Baptist to the end of the chapter. This translation maintains that verse 31 to the end is the voice of the narrator, the Evangelist John, and is a gloss on the preceding statements of the Baptist.

Chapter 4

4:1) As soon as[102] the Lord learned that the Pharisees had received reports saying, "Jesus is making and baptizing more followers than John" – 4:2) although Jesus himself was not performing baptisms, only his students – 4:3) he left Judea and returned to Galilee. 4:4) Jesus had to pass through Samaria,[103] 4:5) and arrived at a town in Samaria called Sychar, near the piece of land that Jacob bequeathed to his son, Joseph. 4:6) Jacob's Well was there, and Jesus, weary from his journey, sat down by the well. It was about the sixth hour.[104] 4:7) A woman of Samaria approached to draw some water.

"Give me a drink," Jesus said to her.[105] 4:8) (His pupils had left for the town to buy some food.)

---

[102] For this expression, *os oun*, see Appendix I.

[103] Samaria is a region between Judea and Galilee, and though it was easier to pass through Samaria to get from one to the other, it was not necessary from a geographical point of view. Samaritans followed a modified version of Judaism and had their own version of the Torah. In Jesus' time, they spurned the Temple, considering Mount Gerizim the focal point of their worship. They were generally looked down upon as ethnically and religiously inferior by their neighbors.

[104] Noon, the same hour as the Crucifixion (19:14).

[105] Rudolf Bultmann cites a parallel from the Buddhist tradition. "Buddha's favorite disciple Ananda, tired after a long journey, asks a girl of the Candala caste who is drawing water at a well for a drink. When she warns him not to contaminate himself, he replies: 'my sister, I do not ask what your caste or your family is; I am only asking you for water, if you can give it to me'." (*The Gospel of John: A Commentary*, trans. G. R. Beasley-Murray (Oxford: Basil Blackwell, 1971), p. 179).

4:9) The Samaritan woman responded, "How is it that you, a Jew, ask me, a Samaritan and a woman no less, for something to drink? Surely, Jews have no dealings with Samaritans!"[106]

4:10) "If you knew the gift of Love," Jesus replied to her, "and who it was that said to you, 'Give me a drink,' you would have asked him and he would have given you living water."

4:11) "Mister," the woman said to him, "you have no bucket to draw water and the cistern is deep, so where are you going to get your *living*[107] water? 4:12) Are you greater than our father Jacob, who gave us the cistern, and drank from it himself, along with his children and his livestock?"

4:13) "Everyone who drinks from this water will thirst again," Jesus answered her. 4:14) "But those who drink of the water that I give them, they will never thirst for evermore. The water that I give to them will become a fountain of water within them, springing up to eternal life."

---

[106] Some translations interpret this last sentence as a comment of the Evangelist. We have retained the voice of the Samaritan Woman, interpreting *ou gar* (Surely ... no) as indicating indignation (Herbert Weir Smyth, *op. cit.,* pg. 638, par. 2805b.).

[107] The same word, *zon* "living," as in 4:10. This is a play on words in which the Samaritan Woman clearly means "running" or "fresh" water, not the standing water of the cistern, and Jesus means something else.

4:15) "Mister," the woman said to him, "give me that water! Then I won't be thirsty anymore or need to keep coming here to draw water."

4:16) "Go get your husband," Jesus said to her, "and come back."

4:17) "I don't have a husband," the woman replied.

Jesus repeated to her, "'I don't have a husband....' Well said! 4:18) The fact is you have had five husbands, and the man you now live with is not your husband. This much you said truthfully."[108]

4:19) "Sir, I perceive you are a prophet," the woman said to him. 4:20) "Our ancestors worshipped on this mountain,[109] but your people say, 'in Jerusalem,' that is the place one should worship."

4:21) "My Lady,[110] believe me," Jesus said to her, "a time is coming when you will worship Love neither on this mountain nor in Jerusalem. 4:22) You Samaritans do not know what you worship; we Jews do know what we worship, because salvation

---

[108] One can imagine Jesus smiling. The ironic humor in Jesus' response is palpable in the original Greek.

[109] Mt. Gerizim. The woman deftly pivots from her personal life to religion.

[110] See footnote 86.

originates from us. 4:23) But a time is coming – and it is now! – when the true worshippers will worship Love in spirit and in truth, for Love seeks such worshippers as these. 4:24) Love is spirit; and those who worship Love must do so in spirit and in truth."

4:25) "I know that the Messiah is coming, the one called 'Christ'," the woman said to him. "When he comes, he will reveal all things to us."

4:26) "I Am,"[111] Jesus said to her, "the one speaking with you."

4:27) Just then, his students came on the scene. They were surprised that Jesus was speaking to a woman. (However, nobody said, "*What* were you looking for?" or "Why were you speaking with *her*?")[112]

4:28) Then, forgetting her water pitcher, the woman ran back to the town, calling to the townsfolk, 4:29) "Come on! See a man who told me everything I have ever done! Is it possible that

---

[111] The capitalization used in this "I Am" indicates the Greek *ego eimi*, which, in the writings of the Apostle John, points to the "Ο ΩΝ" the Divine Name (YHWH) revealed to Moses at the Burning Bush (Exodus 3:14, LXX), often translated, "I AM WHO I AM." The same expression is translated with "I Am" in reference to Christ in the following 22 verses: 6:20,35,41,48,51; 8:12,18,24, 28,58; 10:7,9,11,14; 11:25; 13:19; 14:6; 15:1,5; 18:5,6,8.

[112] There seems to be a hint of scandal in the minds of the disciples, who are not amazed that Jesus is speaking with a Samaritan, but rather with a woman.

this man is the Christ?" 4:30) And they rushed out of the town and were flocking to Jesus.

4:31) In the meantime, his students were pressing him, "Rabbi, eat something."

4:32) "I have food to eat of which you know nothing," Jesus answered them.

4:33) Then his students began asking each other, "Who brought him something to eat?"

4:34) "My nourishment," Jesus said to them, "is to do the will of Love that sent me and to complete Love's work. 4:35) Do you not say, 'Four months to go, and then comes the harvest?' Look, I tell you! Lift up your eyes and look at these fields – how they are already white for the reaping![113] 4:36) Indeed, the reaper is earning his wage and gathering fruit for eternal life, so that both the sower and the reaper rejoice together. 4:37) Here the proverb[114] is true: 'One sows; another reaps.' 4:38) I am sending you on a mission to reap a harvest for which you have not labored. Others did the work, and you have entered into their labor."

---

[113] Wheat that is ripe is golden in color, but it turns pale when left in the field too long. The Samaritans are coming toward them even as Jesus is speaking, just as over-ripe grain falls off the stalk.

[114] This appears to have been a current proverb, although some scholars believe it is a reference to Micah 6:15.

4:39) Many Samaritans of that town believed in Jesus because of the report of the woman, who bore witness, "He told me everything I have ever done." 4:40) As soon as[115] the Samaritans reached Jesus, they asked him to remain with them. Jesus stayed there two days, 4:41) and many more people came to believe in him because of his Message.

4:42) They told the woman, "We no longer believe because of what you told us. For we have heard for ourselves and we know that this man truly is the Christ, the Savior of the world!"

4:43) When the two days were up, Jesus departed and set out for Galilee. 4:44) Indeed, Jesus himself bore witness, "A prophet is not respected in his own homeland." 4:45) When he arrived in Galilee, Galileans, who had also been at the Feast, welcomed him because they had seen the things he had done in Jerusalem during the Passover.[116]

4:46) Then Jesus went back to Cana of Galilee, where he had made the water wine. Down in Capernaum, there was a royal official, whose son had taken ill. 4:47) When he heard that Jesus had come from Judea into Galilee, he set out for him, imploring

---

[115] See Appendix I.
[116] The same Passover as in verse 2:23.

22

him to come down and heal his son; for the boy was on the brink of death.

4:48) "Unless you people see signs and wonders," Jesus said to him, "you will not believe."

4:49) "My lord," the royal official pleaded with him, "you must come before my son dies!"

4:50) "Go your way," Jesus assured him, "your son lives." And the man trusted in the word that Jesus had spoken to him and he went his way. 4:51) On his return, his slaves met him and gave him the news that his son was alive. 4:52) He asked them the time at which his son's health had improved.

"The fever left him yesterday at the seventh hour,"[117] they answered him. 4:53) Then the father knew that it was at the exact time that Jesus had said to him, "Your son lives." And he and his whole household believed. 4:54) This was the second sign Jesus performed when he went back again from Judea into Galilee.

---

[117] One o'clock p.m.

Chapter 5

5:1) Later, Jesus traveled up to Jerusalem for a Jewish religious festival.[118] 5:2) In Jerusalem by the Sheep-Gate, there is a reservoir with five arcades. In the Hebrew language it is called "Bethesda."[119] 5:3) A great mass of the ill and infirm huddled within the arcades. All of them – sightless eyes, weakened knees, withered spirits – waited anxiously for the movement of the water.

5:4)[120] For at just the right moment,[121] an angel would descend into the reservoir, and the water would ripple and undulate. Whoever was first into the water after the rippling effect would be healed, regardless of the disease that afflicted them.

5:5) A certain man was there, gripped by illness for thirty-eight years. 5:6) Jesus saw him prostrate on the ground and knew that the man had been there a very long time.

Jesus asked him, "Do you want to become well?"

---

[118] Most likely, Shavuot (Pentecost), the observance of the revelation of the Law to Moses on Mount Sinai.

[119] "House of Mercy."

[120] This verse, omitted in most manuscripts of the New Testament, is included in *Textus Constantinopolitanus*.

[121] Greek, *kairos.*

5:7) The sick man answered him, "Sir, I have no one to put me in the pool when the water moves. While I inch my way, someone else climbs in before me."

5:8) "Get up," Jesus said to him. "Pick up your cot, and walk." 5:9) That very instant the man was healed, and he picked up his cot and took off walking. But that particular day was Saturday – the Sabbath.

5:10) Some people[122] shouted at the man who had been healed, "It's the Sabbath!"

"It's not lawful for you to carry your cot!"

5:11) The man answered them, "The man who made me well told me, 'Pick up your cot and walk'."

5:12) "What man told you, 'Pick up your cot and walk'?" they demanded of him. 5:13) But the healed man did not know who Jesus was; Jesus had slipped the crowd that filled the place.

5:14) Later, Jesus found him in the Temple and said to him, "See, you have been restored to health. Err no more, lest something worse befall you." 5:15) Then the man went out and declared to the people[123] that it was Jesus who had healed him. 5:16) Indeed,

---

[122] Greek, *Ioudaios*.
[123] *Ibid.*

this was the reason the religious authorities[124] kept persecuting Jesus – even looking for ways to have him condemned to death – because he did these things on the Sabbath.

5:17) But Jesus gave them this answer, "Up until now, it has been Love that has been working. Now, I also am working!"

5:18) This was even more the reason that the religious authorities sought to put Jesus to death. Not only did he unbind the Sabbath, but he said that Love was his Begetter,[125] making himself the equal of Love.

5:19) "Amen, amen, I say to you," Jesus spoke to them, "the Son cannot do anything of himself, only what he sees Love doing. Truly, whatever Love does, the Son does also. 5:20) For Love cherishes the Son, manifesting to him all Her works, and Love will manifest to the Son greater deeds than these, that you may marvel.

5:21) "Truly, as Love raises the dead and imbues them with life, so also the Son endows with life whomsoever he will. 5:22) Love decides for no one, but has delivered judgment to the Son, 5:23) that all may honor the Son even as they honor Love.

---

[124] *Ibid.*
[125] See Introduction, pg. xix.

Whoever honors not the Son honors not Love that sent him. 5:24) Amen, amen, I say to you, whoever hearkens to my Message and believes in the one who sent me has eternal life. And comes not into judgment, but has passed over from death to life. 5:25) Amen, amen, I say to you, the hour is coming and now is, when the dead will hear the voice of the Son of God, and those who hearken will live. 5:26) For just as Love possesses life of Herself, even so She grants the Son to possess life of himself, 5:27) and grants the Son authority, even to pass judgment, because he is the Son of Man.

5:28) "Do not marvel at this, for the hour is coming when all who are in their graves will hear the Son's voice. 5:29) Then those who have done good will come forth to the resurrection of life, and those who have done evil to the resurrection of choice.[126] 5:30) Of myself, I can do nothing. As I hear I decide, and my decision is righteous, because I seek not my own will, but the will of Love that sent me.

5:31) "If I were to bear witness concerning myself, my witness would not be truthful. 5:32) There is another who bears

---

[126] See Introduction, page xxi. Greek, *krisis*, normally means decision or even judgment. "Choice" is used here to show that we have responsibility for the consequences of our actions. See entry in Liddell and Scott, *op. cit.*, pg. 997, A.3.

witness about me, and I know that the testimony declared about me is truthful. 5:33) You sent your delegation to John, and he bore witness honestly.[127] 5:34) But a human attestation? I do not need it.[128] Rather, I tell you these things so that you might be healed.

5:35) "John was a blazing, brilliant lamp, and for a time, you were willing enough to rejoice in his light. 5:36) But the witness I have is greater than John's, for the labors that Love has given me to perfect, these are the very labors I am accomplishing. They bear witness to me that Love has sent me! 5:37) Indeed, Love sent me; She bears witness to me. You never listened to Love's voice. You never beheld Love's beauty. 5:38) And because you do not believe in the one whom Love sent, you do not have Love's Message dwelling inside you.

5:39) "You search the Scriptures because you think that by them you will gain eternal life. Yet the Scriptures are the very things that bear witness to me! 5:40) But you are not willing to come to me that you might possess life. 5:41) To be glorified by people? I do not welcome it.[129] 5:42) But I do know that you do not have the compassionate loving-kindness of Love within you.

---

[127] 1:19 – 28.
[128] Literally, "receive" (Greek, *lambano*).
[129] *Ibid.*

5:43) I come in the name of Love, but you do not accept me. If someone else comes in his own name, him you will accept. 5:44) How will you find the strength to believe, when you continually grasp for praise from each other? You are not even looking for the glory that comes only from Love.

5:45) "Do not think that I will accuse you before Love. You have an accuser, Moses – the very one in whom you placed all your hopes! 5:46) Indeed, if you had believed in Moses, you would have believed in me, for he was writing about me. 5:47) So, if you have no faith in his writings, how are you going to believe in my words?"

Chapter 6

6:1) After this, Jesus departed for the other side of the Sea of Galilee (the Sea of Tiberias). 6:2) A huge throng was following him because they had seen the signs he performed for the sick. 6:3) Jesus climbed up a mountainside and sat down in the midst of his followers. 6:4) (The Jewish feast of Passover[130] was fast approaching.) 6:5) Jesus lifted up his eyes and gazed upon the vast crowds that had come for him.

He asked Philip, "Where are we going to buy the loaves of bread that all these people may have something to eat?" 6:6) (He said this to him in order to prove him. In fact, he already knew what he was going to do.)

6:7) Philip answered him, "Two hundred denarii[131] worth of bread is not going to be enough for them, even for each to have just a bite!"

6:8) One of his disciples, Andrew, the brother of Simon Peter, volunteered, "There is a little boy here with five barley loaves[132] and two fish. Yet what are these for so many?"

---

[130] This is the second Passover mentioned in the Gospel.
[131] The denarius (plural – denarii) was worth a day's wage.
[132] Barley was the least expensive bread.

6:10) Jesus said, "Have the people lie down."[133] There was an abundance of grass in that place. The number of men alone who reclined for the meal was around five thousand.[134]

6:11) Then Jesus took the loaves, and when he had given thanks he gave them to the disciples. And the disciples distributed the loaves to everyone as they reclined. They distributed the fish the same way, giving everyone as much as they wanted. 6:12) When all were sated, Jesus said to his disciples, "Gather up the fragments that remain, that none be lost." 6:13) They gathered up the fragments of the five barley loaves, what remained after everyone had eaten, and filled twelve baskets.

6:14) When the people saw the sign that Jesus did, they cried out, "Truly, this man is the Prophet[135] who has come to the world!" 6:15) Realizing that they were advancing to seize him and declare him a king, Jesus withdrew alone high up the mountain.

---

[133] Reclining for meals was the fashion at the time of Jesus and was the manner of the Supper on the night of his betrayal. In this miracle, as recounted in the Gospel of Mark, there is a further detail that "the disciples arranged everyone like garden plots in groups of fifty and groups of a hundred" (Mark 6:40). The feeding of the five thousand is the only miracle or sign that occurs in all four Gospels.

[134] The crowd estimate does not include the women and children who were also present.

[135] See note 79.

6:16) As evening was falling, his disciples went down to the sea. 6:17) When they boarded their boat it was already dark, and Jesus had not arrived, so they set sail for Capernaum on the far shore of the sea. 6:18) The sea was churning and swelled with strong gusts of wind. 6:19) The disciples had sailed about twenty-five or thirty *stadia*,[136] when they saw Jesus walking on the sea, drawing closer and closer to the boat. They were terrified.

6:20) Jesus called out to them, "I Am.[137] Fear not!" 6:21) They were eager to receive Jesus into the boat, and in a flash, the boat reached the sought-for shore.

6:22) The next morning, the crowd, which had stayed behind on the opposite shore, saw that the boat that his disciples had embarked in (without Jesus) had departed. 6:23) Other boats began arriving from the town of Tiberias, landing near the place where they had eaten the bread over which the Lord had given thanks. 6:24) When the throngs realized that Jesus and his disciples were gone, they boarded these boats and set out for Capernaum

---

[136] Between 3 and 3½ miles, about halfway across. One *stadion* (pl. *stadia*) equals 607 feet. Twenty-five *stadia* would be nearly 3 miles; thirty *stadia* would be almost 3½ miles. The Sea of Galilee is quite large, about 12½ miles from north to south, and 7½ miles east to west at its widest point.
[137] See note 111.

looking for Jesus. 6:25) Finding him on the far shore, they asked him, "Rabbi, when did you get here?"

6:26) "Amen, amen, I say to you," Jesus answered them, "you seek me not because you saw signs, but because you ate of those loaves and your bellies were filled. 6:27) Do not toil for food that perishes, but for the food that abides unto eternal life, which the Son of Man will give you. For the Son of Man bears the seal of the Begetter, Love."

6:28) The people asked him, "What should we do to accomplish the works of God?"

6:29) "This is the work of Love," Jesus answered them, "that you trust in the one whom Love has sent."

6:30) "So what sign are you going to perform, that we may see and believe in you?" they clamored at him. "What are you going to do?" [138]

6:31) "Our ancestors ate manna in the wilderness. As it is written, 'He granted them to eat the bread of heaven.'"[139]

---

[138] In fact, the sign has been accomplished (verses 11-13), but has gone unrecognized. In verse 36, Jesus identifies himself as the sign. This theme of recognition is ubiquitous throughout the Gospel and is explained by the Evangelist in 12:37-41. It may well account for the repeated Homeric trope elsewhere in the Gospel (see Appendix I).

[139] Psalm 78:24, Exodus chapter 16.

6:32) "Amen, amen, I say to you," Jesus addressed them, "it was not Moses who gave you the bread of heaven; rather, it is Love that gives you the true bread of heaven. 6:33) Truly, the bread of Love is the one who descends from heaven, granting life to the world."

6:34) "Sir, give us this bread all the time!" they implored him,

6:35) "I Am[140] the bread of life!" Jesus exclaimed to them. "Whoever comes to me will never ever hunger, and whoever believes in me will never ever thirst! 6:36) But I have been telling you; you have seen me, and still you do not believe![141]

6:37) "All that Love has bestowed upon me will come to me, and I will never cast out the one who comes to me, 6:38) because I descended from heaven, not to accomplish my own will, but the will of Love that sent me. 6:39) And this is the will of Love that sent me, that I should lose none of all that are given to me, but rather I should raise them up at the Last Day. 6:40) This is the will

---

[140] See note 111.

[141] Some commentaries insist that the word "me" should not be included (as it is missing from certain Greek manuscripts) and that the sense of the passage is "even though you have seen (the signs in 6:26), you do not believe." In *Textus Constantinopolitanus*, the "me" is included. Jesus is the sign the people have been seeking, neither the bread that fed the five thousand, nor the manna in the wilderness.

of the Love that sent me, that everyone who beholds the Son and believes in him might have eternal life, and I will raise them up at the Last Day."

6:41) Then some of the people[142] started grumbling about him, because he said, 'I Am[143] the bread that descends out of Heaven.'

6:42) "Isn't this Jesus, the son of Joseph?" some were saying.

"Don't we know his father and his mother?"

"How can he say, 'I have descended from heaven'?"

6:43) Jesus challenged them, "Stop your murmuring. 6:44) None are able to come to me, unless Love that sent me draws them, and I will raise them up on the Last Day. 6:45) It is written in the Prophets, 'And they shall all be instructed by Love.'[144] Every person who listens and learns from Love comes to me." 6:46)[145] (Not that anyone has seen Love. Only HE WHO IS[146] from Love has seen Love.)

---

[142] Greek, *Ioudaios*.
[143] See note 111.
[144] Isaiah 54:13 (adapted).
[145] Verse 46 is an aside of the Evangelist. Jesus resumes at verse 47.
[146] See note 77.

6:47) "Amen, amen, I say to you, the one who believes in me possesses eternal life. 6:48) I Am[147] the bread of life! 6:49) Your ancestors ate manna in the wilderness and they died. 6:50) This is the bread who descends from heaven, so that any who feed on him might never die. 6:51) I Am[148] the living bread that descended from heaven! If any feed on this bread, they shall live forevermore. And what is more, the bread that I shall give is my flesh, which I offer for the life of the world."

6:52) "How can this man give us his flesh to eat?" they[149] said, and a quarrel broke out among them.

6:53) "Amen, amen, I say to you," Jesus continued, "unless you feed on the flesh of the Son of Man and drink his blood, you have no life within. 6:54) Those who feed on my flesh and drink my blood possess eternal life, and I will raise them up at the Last Day. 6:55) Indeed, my flesh is truly a food that nourishes and my blood is truly a drink that quenches. 6:56) Those who feed on my flesh and drink my blood abide in me and I in them. 6:57) Just as living Love sent me and I live because of Love, the one who feeds on me will live because of me. 6:58) This is the bread that

---

[147] See note 111.
[148] *Ibid.*
[149] Greek, *Ioudaios.*

descended from heaven, unlike the manna your ancestors ate. They died. The one who feeds on this bread will live forevermore." 6:59) Jesus said these things while teaching in the synagogue at Capernaum.

6:60) Then many of his own students who had been listening began to mutter, "This teaching[150] is confusing."

"Who can listen to this?"

6:61) Jesus realized that even his own students were grumbling over what he had said and he reproved them, "Does this scandalize you? 6:62) Then what if you were to see the Son of Man ascending to the place he was before? 6:63) The spirit creates life! The flesh profits nothing. The words[151] I say to you, they are spirit and they are life! 6:64) But there are some among you who do not believe." (For Jesus knew from the beginning that there would be some who would not believe, and who it was who would betray him.) 6:65) He continued, "This is the reason that I told you that none of you are able to come unto me, unless it is granted to you by Love."

---

[150] Greek, *logos.*
[151] Greek, *rhema.*

6:66) As a result of this teaching, many of his followers turned back and no longer walked after him.

6:67) Then Jesus asked the Twelve, "Do you also want to leave?"

6:68) "Lord," Simon Peter answered him, "Where would we go? You have the words of eternal life! 6:69) We *do* believe, and we know that you are the Christ! The Son of Living Love!"

6:70) "Is it not I who chose the twelve of you?" Jesus replied. "And is not one of you a devil?"

6:71) Jesus was speaking about Judas Iscariot, the son of Simon, because it was he – one of the Twelve – who would betray him.

Chapter 7

7:1) After these events, Jesus spent his time in the countryside of Galilee. He did not wish to travel to Judea because the religious authorities[152] were on the lookout for him, seeking to put him to death.

7:2) The Jewish Feast of Tabernacles[153] was fast approaching 7:3) and Jesus' brothers[154] said to him, "You should leave here and get back to Judea."

"So your students can see the exploits you perform!"

7:4) "Who does something in secret if they are looking to be in the public eye?"

"If you *are* doing these exploits, show yourself to the world!"

7:5) Not even his own brothers believed in him. 7:6) Jesus said to them, "My time[155] is not quite here, but your time is always at hand. 7:7) The world cannot hate you, but it hates me because I bear witness that its deeds are evil. 7:8) Go ahead, go up for the feast. I am not going up for this feast, for my time is not yet

---

[152] Greek, *Ioudaios*.
[153] Mid-to late October. The Feast of Tabernacles (Hebrew, Sukkoth) remains the setting through 10:22.
[154] See note 89.
[155] Greek, *kairos*.

complete." 7:9) This is what Jesus said to them, and he remained behind in Galilee. 7:10) However, once his brothers had departed, he did go up for the feast, but not openly – in secret.

7:11) The Judeans[156] were looking for Jesus during the festival, asking, "Where is that man?" 7:12) Undercurrents flowed through the crowd about him. "He is a good man," some were saying.

Others protested, "Wrong! He deceives the masses." 7:13) Yet, nobody spoke openly about Jesus, because they were afraid of the religious authorities.[157]

7:14) It was already mid-way through the Feast when Jesus went up into the Temple and began to teach. 7:15) Some of the people[158] were bewildered and wondered aloud, "How can this man with no schooling have such a grasp of Scripture?"

7:16) Jesus answered them, "My teaching is not mine, but of Love that sent me. 7:17) If you desire to do the will of Love, you will recognize the teaching, whether it is of Love, or whether I am speaking of myself. 7:18) Those who speak of themselves seek their own fame, but he who seeks the glory of the one who sent

---

[156] Greek, *Ioudaios.*

[157] *Ibid.*

[158] *Ibid.*

him, he is truthful and there is no unrighteousness in him. 7:19) Did not Moses give you the Law? Yet, there is not one among you who observes the Law. Why are you trying to kill me?"

7:20) "You're mad!" people in the crowd shouted.

"Possessed!"

"Who's trying to kill you?"

7:21) Jesus defended himself to them, "I performed one deed,[159] and all of you are amazed because of it. 7:22) Moses gave you circumcision, not that it originated with Moses, but with the patriarchs.[160] Yet, you circumcise a man on the Sabbath. 7:23) Now if a man can receive circumcision on the Sabbath so as not to annul the Law of Moses, why are you angry with me because I healed an entire man on the Sabbath? 7:24) Do not pass judgment according to appearance, but pass a righteous judgment."

7:25) There was much talk among local citizens of Jerusalem: "Isn't this the man they are trying to kill?"

7:26) "And look, he is speaking out in the open and no one is challenging him!"

---

[159] The healing of the man at the Pool of Bethesda in chapter 5.
[160] Literally, "fathers."

"Could it be that the authorities really know that this man truly is the Messiah?"

7:27) "But we know where he comes from, and when the Messiah comes, no one will know where he comes from!"

7:28) Jesus cried aloud as he taught in the Temple, "So, you not only know me, you know where I come from! Yet, I have not come of myself. But Love that sent me is true. You do not know Love. 7:29) I know Love, because I am from Love! Love has sent me."

7:30) Then some men attempted to seize Jesus, but no one laid a hand on him, because his hour had not yet come. 7:31) Nevertheless, many in the crowd were starting to believe in him. People were saying, "When the Messiah arrives, is he going to do greater signs than this man does?"

7:32) The Pharisees heard these stirrings of the crowd about Jesus and they, together with the Chief Priests, dispatched their subordinates[161] to arrest him.

---

[161] The constabulary of the Temple.

7:33) "Just a little more time I am with you," Jesus continued. "Then I go to Love that sent me. 7:34) You will seek me, but you will not find me. And where I am, you cannot come."

7:35) "Where is he off to?" people[162] were saying among themselves, "that we won't be able to find him?"

"Could he be going to the Diaspora[163] among the Greeks, and teach the Greeks?"

7:36) "What did he mean when he said, 'You will seek me, but you will not find me'? And, 'where I am, you cannot come'?"

7:37) On the last and most important day of the Feast,[164] Jesus stood up and cried aloud, "If you thirst, come to me and drink! 7:38) Those who believe in me, as the Scripture says, 'Out of the deepest chambers of their being shall rush forth rivers of living water'!"[165]

7:39) (Now Jesus said this concerning the Spirit that was to be received by those who believed in him. For the Holy Spirit was not yet, because Jesus had not yet entered into his glory.)

---

[162] Greek, *Ioudaios*.

[163] The Diaspora (dispersion) was the Jewish community that lived outside of Israel. There were communities in Greece, Asia Minor, Alexandria, Rome, and beyond. Their language was Greek, the *lingua franca* of the Roman Empire.

[164] Simchat Torah, which means, "Rejoicing in the Torah." This was the day before the commencement of the reading of the Torah for the year.

[165] Cf. Proverbs 18:4

7:40) After they heard Jesus say this, many from the crowd exclaimed, "This man really *is* the Prophet!"

7:41) Others cried out, "This man is the Christ!"

"What now!" others retorted, "The Messiah comes from Galilee?"

7:42) "Doesn't the Scripture state that the Messiah is of the lineage of David?"[166]

"And comes from Bethlehem, the village of David?"[167]

7:43) And there was a deep division in the crowd over him. 7:44) Some people wanted to seize him, but nobody laid a hand on him.

7:45) When their subordinates returned, the Chief Priests and the Pharisees accosted them, "Why didn't you arrest him?"

7:46) "No man ever spoke like this man," they answered.

7:47) The Pharisees lashed out at them, "Not you too!"

"So you are deceived as well?"

7:48) "Have any of the leadership believed in him? Any of the Pharisees?"

---

[166] Cf. II Samuel 7:12.
[167] Cf. Micah 5:2.

7:49) "But no! This mob that knows nothing of the Law! They're even more accursed!"

7:50) Nikodemos, who was one of them, the same one who came to Jesus at night,[168] spoke up in front of them all, 7:51) "Does our Law judge a person if it has not first listened to him and has an understanding of his actions?"

7:52) "Are you from Galilee as well?" the Pharisees shot back.

"Search and see – no prophet arises out of Galilee!"

7:53) Then each one went off to their own home.

---

[168] 3:1-22.

Chapter 8

8:1)[169] Jesus retired to the Mount of Olives. 8:2) In the morning, he returned to the Temple and all the people rushed to him. He took his seat and was beginning to teach the people, 8:3) when the Scribes[170] and the Pharisees pushed their way in, dragging a woman who had been caught in the act of adultery.

They shoved her in front of everyone 8:4) calling to Jesus, "Rabbi, this woman was caught red-handed committing adultery!"

8:5) "And in *our* Law Moses commands such people to be stoned."

"What do *you* say?" 8:6) (Their question was meant to trap him, to fabricate an accusation against him.)

Jesus stooped down and started writing with his finger in the dirt.[171] 8:7) His inquisitors were not budging.

Jesus raised his head and said, "Whoever is without fault among you, you be the first to cast a stone at her." 8:8) Then he stooped down again and resumed writing in the dirt.

---

[169] Textus Criticus does not have the story of the woman caught in adultery (through 8:11), and in addition is missing the previous verse, 7:53.

[170] This is the only occurrence of the word, *grammateus* – scribe, in this Gospel.

[171] The only report of Jesus ever writing anything; the content is not recorded.

8:9) When they heard this, one by one they shuffled off, starting with the older men first. The woman did not move from the spot where they thrust her. Jesus was the only one remaining.

8:10) Jesus lifted his head and addressed the woman, "My Lady,[172] where are they? Has anyone condemned you?"

8:11) "No one, Sir," she quavered.

"And I do not condemn you either." Jesus said. "Go your way and from this moment, sin no more."

8:12) Jesus addressed the people again, saying, "I Am[173] the light of the world. Whoever follows me will not walk in darkness, but will have the light of life."

8:13) Some Pharisees accosted him, "So you do bear witness to yourself!"

"Your witness is not honest!"

8:14) Jesus answered them, "Even if I did bear witness to myself, my witness would be honest, because I know where I come from and I know where I am going. 8:15) You make judgments based on the flesh. I judge no one.[174] 8:16) But if I were to pass judgment, my judgment would be true, because I am not alone. I

---

[172] See note 86.
[173] See note 111.
[174] Cf. 8:11.

am with Love that sent me. 8:17) Even in your Law it is written that the witness of two persons is reliable. 8:18) I Am[175] one who bears witness to myself, and Love that sent me bears witness to me."

8:19) "Where is your *Love?*" they asked him.

"You neither know me, nor Love," Jesus replied. "If you had known me, you would have known Love as well." 8:20) Jesus spoke these words by one of the Temple collection boxes, as he was teaching in the Temple compound, but no one tried to seize him, because his hour had not yet come. 8:21) Jesus addressed them again, "I am going, and you will search for me, and you will die in your error. Where I am going, you cannot come."

8:22) "Maybe he's going to kill himself," some people[176] said.

"He did say, 'Where I am going, you cannot come'."

8:23) Jesus continued, "You are from below. I am from above. You are of this world. I am not of this world. 8:24) That is

---

[175] See note 111.
[176] Greek, *Ioudaios.*

why I said to you that you will die in your sins. For if you do not believe that I Am,[177] you will die in your sins."

8:25) "Who *are* you?" they demanded of him.

"Even what I told you from the beginning," Jesus replied. 8:26) "I have many things to say about you and to decide, but the one who sent me is truthful. The things that I have heard from Love, these are the things I speak to the world." 8:27) (They did not understand that he spoke to them of Love.) 8:28) Then Jesus said to them, "When you exalt the Son of Man, then you will know that I Am,[178] and that I do nothing of myself. What I say is as Love teaches me. 8:29) Love sent me and is with me. Love has not left me alone, because I always do the things that are pleasing to Love."

8:30) When Jesus had said this, many began to put their faith in him. 8:31) Jesus continued speaking to the people[179] who were coming to believe in him, "If you abide in my Message, then you are truly my followers. 8:32) And you will know the truth, and the truth will set you free."

---

[177] See note 111.
[178] *Ibid.*
[179] Greek, *Ioudaios.*

8:33) Some of them protested to him, "We are the seed and heirs of Abraham!"

"We have never been enslaved to anyone!"

"How can you say to us, 'you will be free'?"

8:34) "Amen, amen, I say to you," Jesus replied to them, "everyone who sins is a slave to sin. 8:35) The slave does not remain in the house forever, but the Son abides forever. 8:36) Therefore, if the Son makes you free, you are truly free. 8:37) I know that you are the progeny of Abraham, but you seek to kill me, because there is no room inside you for my Message. 8:38) I tell you that which I have seen of Love. And in truth, you do that which you have seen from your father."

8:39) "Our father is Abraham!" they shouted at him.

"If your father were Abraham," Jesus said to them, "you would do the deeds of Abraham. 8:40) But now you seek to put me to death, a man who spoke the truth to you, the truth that I heard from Love. This, Abraham would not do! 8:41) You do the deeds of your father."

"We were not born of a whore!"[180] they shot back at him. "We have a father, God!"

8:42) "If Love were your Parent," Jesus said to them, "you would have loved and cherished me, for I came forth from Love and am here now! I did not even come of myself; Love sent me. 8:43) Why do you not understand what I am saying? Because you cannot bear to hear my Message. 8:44) You are of your father, the devil! And you want to fulfill his lusts. From the beginning, he was a murderer, a slayer of humankind. He never could stand the truth, because there is no truth in him. Whenever he opens his mouth he is lying, because he is a liar who sires liars. 8:45) But I, because I tell you the truth, you do not believe me. 8:46) Who among you will expose fault in me? So, if I am speaking the truth, why not put your faith in me? 8:47) A person who is of Love listens to the words of Love. This is why you do not listen, because you are not of Love."

8:48) "O, how right we were to say that you are a Samaritan and a demoniac!" they[181] snapped back at him.

---

[180] Literally, prostitution (Greek, *porneia*); this harsh remark may have reflected current ambiguities about the circumstances of Jesus' birth.
[181] Greek, *Ioudaios*.

8:49) "I am not possessed by some demon," Jesus replied, "rather, I honor Love, but you dishonor me. 8:50) And I do not seek my own glory. There is one who seeks and who judges. 8:51) Amen, amen, I say to you, those who hold to my Message shall never, ever see death!"

8:52) They[182] railed at Jesus, "Now we know you have a demon!"

"Abraham is dead."

"The prophets are dead."

"Yet you say, 'Anyone who keeps my word shall never, ever taste death'."

8:53) "Are you greater than our father, Abraham, who died?"

"And the prophets, who died?"

"Who do you make yourself out to be?"

8:54) Jesus answered, "If I glorify myself, my glory is nothing. There is one that glorifies me, Love, whom you say is your God. 8:55) Yet, you do not know Love. I *do* know Love. If I said I did not know Love, I would be like you, a liar. But I do

---

[182] *Ibid.*

know Love and I keep Love's word. 8:56) Your father Abraham

rejoiced to see my day. He not only saw it, he saw it and was

glad."

8:57) "You are not even fifty years old!"[183] they[184]

challenged him, "and you have seen Abraham?"

8:58) "Before Abraham was, I Am,"[185] Jesus replied to

them.

8:59) Then they picked up stones to hurl at him, but Jesus

hid, and left the Temple making his way right through the midst of

them.

---

[183] This is not so much a reference to Jesus' age as it is to a Biblical standard of
maturity (cf. Number 4:3).
[184] Greek, *Ioudaios*.
[185] See note 111.

Chapter 9[186]

9:1) As Jesus passed by, he noticed a man blind from birth.

9:2) "Rabbi," his students asked him, "who was at fault, that he was born blind?"

"The man himself?"

"Or his parents?"

9:3) "No one is at fault," Jesus responded, "neither the man nor his parents. He was born blind so that Love's deeds might manifest in him. 9:4) For my part, I must accomplish the works of the one that sent me while it is yet the day. Night is coming when no one can work. 9:5) Yet, as long as I am in the world, I am the light of the world."

9:6) Jesus left off speaking and spit on the ground making a mixture of mud with his saliva. Then he anointed the eyes of the blind man with the mud, like a physician's plaster. 9:7) Jesus spoke to the blind man, "Go now; wash in the pool of Siloam." ("Siloam" translated means "the apostle, the one sent"). The blind man went off, washed, and came back with his sight.

---

[186] The chapter break does not indicate a break in the action. Jesus has left the Temple precincts, but is still in Jerusalem.

9:8) There was talk in the neighborhood, especially among the people who had seen the man when he was blind, "Isn't that the fellow who used to sit and beg?"

9:9) "It is him!" some said.

"It just looks like him," still others said,

"It *is* me!" the man himself declared.

9:10) Then they asked him, "How were your eyes opened?"

9:11) "A man named Jesus," he answered them, "he mixed up some mud and smeared it on my eyes. Then he told me, 'Go to the pool of Siloam and wash.' So I went, and I washed, and now I see!"

9:11) "Where is this man?" they demanded of him.

"I don't know," he answered.

9:13) These same neighbors hauled the man who had been blind off to the Pharisees. 9:14) (For it was the Sabbath when Jesus made the clay mixture and opened the man's eyes.) 9:15) Then the Pharisees questioned the man again about how he gained his sight.

The man replied to them, "He put mud on my eyes, then I washed it off, and I see!"

9:16) "This man is not from God," some of the Pharisees pronounced, "because he does not observe the Sabbath."

But others wondered, "How is it possible for a man, a sinner, to do such signs?" And a deep rift split the Pharisees.

9:17) The Pharisees questioned the man born blind again, "What do you say about him, seeing that he opened your eyes?"

"He is a prophet," the man answered.

9:18) The authorities[187] did not believe that the man who could now see had once been blind until they called his parents. 9:19) They questioned them. "Is this man your son, the one whom you maintain was born blind? So how is it that he can now see?"

9:20) "We are positive this is our son," they answered, "and that he was born blind. 9:21) But how he can now see, or who opened his eyes, we do not know. He is of age; ask him. He can speak for himself."

9:22) (His parents said this because they were afraid of the religious authorities.[188] The authorities[189] had already agreed to expel from the synagogue anyone who publicly acknowledged

---

[187] Greek, *Ioudaios*.
[188] *Ibid.*
[189] *Ibid.*

Jesus as the Messiah. 9:23) This is the reason why the man's parents said, "He is of age; ask him.")

9:24) The religious authorities then summoned the man who had been blind a second time. "Come on now," they railed at him.

"Give God the glory!"

"We know that this man is a sinner!"

9:25) The man answered them thus, "Whether he is a sinner or not, I don't know. One thing I do know is this: I was blind, but now I see."

9:26) "What did he do to you?" they insisted again.

"How did he open your eyes?"

9:27) "I already told you," he pleaded with them, "and you did not listen. What? Do you want to hear it again? Maybe you want to become his students too?"

9:28) "Go ahead and follow him!" the Pharisees brutally berated him.

"We are followers of Moses!"

9:29) "We know that God spoke to Moses, but this man, we have no idea where he's from."

9:30) "Now isn't that something!" the man retorted. "You have no idea where he came from and yet he opened my eyes. 9:31) But we know that God does not listen to sinners. However, if someone is devout, has a deep reverence for God, and accomplishes his will, God will listen to that kind of person. 9:32) From time immemorial, no one has ever heard of somebody opening the eyes of a man born blind! 9:33) If he were not of God, he could not do anything."

9:34) "You?" they tore into him.

"You were born a sinner!"

"And you dare to instruct us?" And they cast him out.

9:35) Jesus heard that they had expelled the man and he went to find him. "Do you believe in the Son of Love?" Jesus asked him.

9:36) "Who is he, Sir, that I might believe in him?" the man answered him.

9:37) "You have not only seen him," Jesus said to him, "he is the very one speaking with you."

9:38) "I do believe, O Lord!" the man declared, and he fell down in worship before Jesus.

9:39) Jesus continued, "I have come to this world for a decisive judgment, so that those who do not see might gain their sight, and those who do might become blind."

9:40) Some of the Pharisees who were in the vicinity of Jesus overheard him and said, "What? Are we blind as well?"

9:41) Jesus answered them, "If you were blind, you would have no guilt. But then you say, 'We see!' Therefore, your guilt remains."

Chapter 10[190]

10:1) "Amen, amen, I say to you, the one who enters the sheepfold not through the gate, but climbs over some other way, he is a thief and an outlaw. 10:2) But the one who enters through the gate, he is the shepherd of the sheep. 10:3) To him the gatekeeper opens and the sheep hear his voice. He calls his own sheep by name and he leads them forth. 10:4) And whenever he drives his flock of sheep, he goes before them to lead them. His sheep will follow him, because they know the sound of his voice. 10:5) But they will not follow an intruder; rather they flee from him, because they do not recognize the sound of strangers' voices." 10:6) (Jesus related this parable about the Pharisees, but they did not realize that he was speaking about them.)

10:7) "Amen, amen, I say to you," Jesus addressed the people again, "I Am[191] the gate of the sheep. 10:8) All who came before me are thieves and outlaws. 10:9) I Am[192] the gate! Whoever enters through me will be healed, and will enter in, and will go forth, and will find pasture for grazing. 10:10) The thief

---

[190] Again, the chapter break does not indicate a break in the action (see 10:6). Jesus continues to address the people.
[191] See note 111.
[192] *Ibid.*

comes only to steal, to slaughter, and to destroy. I have come so that you might have life and have it abundantly!

10:11) "I Am[193] the good shepherd. The good shepherd sacrifices[194] his life[195] for the sake of the sheep. 10:12) But the hired hand – who is not a shepherd and to whom the sheep do not belong – he sees the wolf coming, deserts the sheep, and runs away. Then the wolf plunders the sheep at will and scatters them like the wind. 10:13) Yes, the hired hand runs away, because he acts only for money and cares not for the sheep.

10:14) "I Am[196] the good shepherd, and I know mine and am known by mine, 10:15) just as Love knows me, and I know Love. And I sacrifice my life for the sake of the sheep. 10:16) I also have other sheep, who are not of this sheepfold. I must go to

---

[193] *Ibid.*

[194] The Greek word *tithemi* has the basic meaning of "to place" and is often translated in this instance as to "lay down" or to "give up." Both meanings seem inadequate to the translators. Placing one's life on the line is an active and purposeful action and it seems better rendered by the English "to sacrifice." And so in 10:15 and 10:17 as well. A similar usage in 1 John 3:16 shows that the sacrifice can mean unto death, but not necessarily so. In 19:40,42 and 20:2,13,15, *tithemi* is used with the meaning to bury, an ancient usage (e.g., as a noun in *The Persians*, line 405).

[195] Greek, *psyche,* principally means "life," but can also mean "soul," as opposed to *zoe,* which means "life" in general and "eternal life" in the writings of John.

[196] See note 111.

them as well. They will hear my voice and there shall be one flock, one shepherd.

10:17) "This is why Love cherishes me, because I sacrifice my life, that I may take it again. 10:18) No one strips my life from me! I sacrifice my life of my own accord. I have the authority to sacrifice it, and I have the authority to take it again. This is the commandment I received from Love."

10:19) Then there was more division among the local people[197] because of these teachings. 10:20) Many were saying, "He is possessed, a madman!"

"Why do you listen to him?"

10:21) But others were saying, "Are these words the words of a demoniac?"

"Could someone who is possessed open the eyes of the blind?"

10:22)[198] Winter arrived and it was the Feast of the Reconsecration[199] in Jerusalem. 10:23) Jesus was walking in the Portico of Solomon within the Temple grounds.

---

[197] Greek, *Ioudaios*.
[198] Here begins a new episode.
[199] The Feast of Lights, Hanukkah.

10:24) Then a group[200] encircled him. "How long are you going to string us along?" they accosted him.

"Pushing our very souls to the brink?"

"If you are the Messiah, tell us outright!"

10:25) "I have told you," Jesus responded, "yet you do not believe. The works that I perform, I do in the name of Love, and these bear witness to me. 10:26) But you do not have faith, for you do not belong to my sheep, as I already told you.[201] 10:27) My sheep listen to my voice, and they follow me. 10:28) Indeed, I will grant them eternal life, and they will never, ever perish. No one will fleece them out of my hand! 10:29) Love has given them to me, and Love is greater than everyone and everything. No one can seize from Love's hand. 10:30) Love and I, we are one."

10:31) Again, some of the people[202] picked up rocks to stone him.[203]

---

[200] Greek, *Ioudaios*.

[201] Cf. 10:4. Textus Criticus omits this last phrase, even though it is well attested, because there appears to be no corresponding quote referenced in the text. However, 10:4 provides the essential material, the contrast of the sheep who do believe, who follow the Good Shepherd, because they "know the sound of his voice."

[202] Greek, *Ioudaios*.

[203] Cf. 8:59.

10:32) Jesus appealed to them "I have shown you many excellent works that come from Love. For which one are you going to stone me?"

10:33) "We won't stone you for some good deed!" they[204] shot back.

"This is for sacrilege!"

"For blasphemy!"

"And because you..."

"A mere mortal!"

"Make yourself out to be God!"

10:34) Jesus challenged them, "Is it not written in your Law, 'I have said, You are gods?'[205] 10:35) If they are called 'gods,' those people to whom the Word of Love came,[206] and the Scripture cannot be annulled, 10:36) then why do you say to me, the one whom Love has consecrated and sent to the world, 'You are committing blasphemy,' when I say I am the Son of Love? 10:37) If I am not accomplishing the works of Love, then do not believe me. 10:38) But if I am, and you still do not believe in me, then believe for the sake of the deeds themselves, so that you may

---

[204] Greek, *Ioudaios*.
[205] Psalm 82:6.
[206] Greek, *pros ous o Logos tou Theou egeneto*.

know and believe that Love is deep within me and I am deep within Love."

10:39) At this they made another attempt to seize him, but he eluded their grasp. 10:40) Jesus withdrew again back beyond the Jordan, to the place where John had first baptized, and remained there. 10:41) Many people came to Jesus, saying that even though John had not given a sign, nevertheless, everything that John had said about Jesus was true. 10:42) And many of the people there began to believe in Jesus.

Chapter 11

11:1) Now a certain man fell gravely ill, Lazaros of Bethany,[207] from the village of Mary and her sister Martha. 11:2) Mary was the woman who anointed the Lord with myrrh and wiped his feet dry with her hair.[208] Lazaros, who had fallen ill, was her brother.

11:3) The sisters sent word to Jesus, "Lord, if you could only see how your dear friend suffers in his sickness."

11:4) When Jesus heard this he said, "This illness is not unto death, but for the glory of Love, that the Son of Love might be glorified through it." 11:5) (Jesus loved Martha, her sister, and Lazaros.) 11:6) But when[209] Jesus heard that Lazaros was ill, he remained exactly where he was for two more days. 11:7) Then, after the two days, he announced to his disciples, "Let us go again into Judea."

11:8) "Rabbi," the disciples said to him, "the Judeans[210] are looking for you even now to stone you to death."

"And you would go there again?"

---

[207] This Bethany is a village over the Mount of Olives, about two miles from Jerusalem.
[208] John 12:3.
[209] See Appendix I.
[210] Greek, *Ioudaios*.

11:9) "Are there not twelve hours of daylight?" Jesus answered. "If any of you walk in the daylight, you will not stumble, because you behold the light of this world. 11:10) But if you walk in the darkness of night, you will stumble because the light is not in you." 11:11) A little while after he said these things Jesus told them, "Lazaros, our friend, has fallen asleep. But I go to wake him."

11:12) "Lord," his disciples said, "if he is sleeping, then he is getting better." 11:13) (But Jesus had spoken of his death; the disciples thought that he was speaking about the slumber of dreams.)

11:14) Then Jesus told them bluntly, "Lazarus is dead. 11:15) And for your sakes I am glad I was not there, that you might believe. But let us go to him."

11:16) Thomas, called the "Twin,"[211] blurted out to his fellow disciples, "Let us go also that we may die with him!"

11:17) When Jesus arrived he found that Lazaros was already four days in the tomb. 11:18) Bethany was close to

---

[211] Greek, *Didymos*. This is the first mention of Thomas in this Gospel. His momentary enthusiasm will later turn to cynical skepticism (20:25).

Jerusalem, about fifteen stadia,[212] 11:19) and many of its inhabitants[213] had come to support Martha and Mary, consoling them in the loss of their brother. 11:20) When Martha learned that Jesus had arrived, she went out to meet him. But Mary sat motionless at home.

11:21) Martha faced Jesus and said to him, "Lord, if you had been here, my brother would not have died. 11:22) But even now I know that whatever you ask of Love, Love will grant it to you."

11:23) "Your brother will rise." Jesus said to her.

11:24) "I know he will." Martha replied to him. "He will rise again at the resurrection on the Last Day."

11:25) "I Am[214] the resurrection and the life!" Jesus declared to her. 11:26) "Those who believe in me, even if they die, they shall live. And everyone who lives in me and believes in me shall never, ever die. Do you believe this?"

11:27) "Yes, Lord!" she cried out. "I have believed and I do believe that you are the Anointed One – the Christ – the Son of Love come to the world!" 11:28) After she said this, she ran back

---

[212] A little under two miles.
[213] Greek, *Ioudaios.*
[214] See note 111.

and called her sister, Mary. "The Rabbi is here," Martha whispered to her, "and he is asking for you." 11:29) As soon as Mary heard this, she immediately rose up and went to Jesus.

11:30) Jesus had not yet entered the village, but was in the exact spot where Martha had met him. 11:31) So when the Judeans[215] who had been consoling Mary in the house saw how quickly she got up and departed, they followed her, saying, "She's going to the tomb to mourn."

11:32) Then Mary came to the place where Jesus was. When she saw him, she fell down at his feet. "Lord," she ached before him, "if you had been here, my brother would not be dead."

11:33) When Jesus saw her weeping, and the Judeans[216] who had accompanied her wailing with grief, he shuddered in his spirit, overcome by emotion, shaken deep within.

11:34) "Where did you bury him?" Jesus asked.

"Lord," Martha began.

"Come and see," Mary finished.[217]

11:35) Jesus wept.

---

[215] Greek, *Ioudaios*.

[216] *Ibid.*

[217] This sentence with one plural verb indicates both sisters responded to Jesus. Breaking the sentence into their two voices seems to correspond to the powerful emotional content.

11:36) "See how he loved him!" people[218] were saying.

11:37) But a few took exception, "Could not this man, who opened the eyes of the blind, have done something to save Lazaros from dying?"

11:38) Then Jesus, again convulsed by profound shudders, halted before the tomb. 11:39) It was a cave. A stone covered it.

"Away with the stone!" Jesus commanded.

Martha, the sister of the dead man, resisted him. "Lord, by now there will be a putrid stench. He has been dead *four* days."

11:40) "Did I not say to you that if you believed, you would see the glory of Love?" Jesus reminded her. 11:41) Then the men removed the stone where the dead man was laid to rest. Lifting his gaze on high Jesus said, "Love, I give you thanks for hearkening to me. 11:42) But I know that you have always heard me. Nevertheless, for the sake of the multitude present – that they might believe that you have sent me – I speak." 11:43) As Jesus finished these words, he rent the air with a mighty cry, "Lazaros! Come forth!"

---

[218] Greek, *Ioudaios.*

11:44) And Lazaros, who to that very moment was dead, emerged with his hands and feet bound together by the charnel linens.[219] His face also had been tightly wrapped and was covered by the face-shroud.[220]

"Loose him and let him go!" Jesus commanded the bystanders.

11:45) Many of the Judeans who had come to comfort Mary saw what Jesus did, and began to believe in him. 11:46) But there were others who ran back to tell the Pharisees what Jesus had done.

11:47) Then the Chief Priests and Pharisees held a meeting of the Sanhedrin where many spoke up. "What are we going to do?"

"Because of the signs this man performs...."

11:48) "If we let him go, everybody is going to end up believing in him!"

---

[219] Greek, *keiria*; a rare word meaning the winding bandages that were part of Jewish funerary rites, similar to what one thinks of with mummies. This unique usage in the New Testament seems to highlight the difference between the entombment and resurrection of Lazaros and that of Jesus (20:6,7), where the word for the same item is *othonia*, translated as "grave-linens."

[220] The *soudarion*, a cloth about the size of a handkerchief, used to cover the face of the deceased in burial (cf. 20:7).

"Then the Romans will come and they'll take away our best rank and station!"[221]

"Indeed our whole nation!"

11:49) Then one of them, Caiaphas, the High Priest for the cycle of that year,[222] launched into them all. "You people don't know anything! 11:50) Haven't you figured out that this is in our interest? Let one man die for the people, rather than the entire nation perish." 11:51) (He did not say this of himself, but as High Priest of the cycle of that year he prophesied that Jesus would die for the nation, 11:52) and not only for the sake of the nation, but so that the children of Love scattered abroad might be gathered into one.) 11:53) From that day, they conspired to put Jesus to death.

11:54) Consequently, Jesus no longer walked openly among the Judeans.[223] Rather, he withdrew from there to an area close to the desert, to a town called Ephraim.[224] There, Jesus passed the time with his disciples.

---

[221] For *ton topon* ("place"); from Hamlet, Act 1, scene 3.

[222] Caiaphas was High Priest from 18 – 36 AD.

[223] Greek, *Ioudaios*.

[224] Most scholars agree a town some ten to twelve miles north of Jerusalem.

11:55) The Jewish Passover[225] was drawing closer. Crowds were coming up from the countryside to Jerusalem to ritually purify themselves before the Passover. 11:56) They milled about in the Temple, looking for Jesus, talking among themselves, "How does it look to you?"

"Do you think he will come for the Feast?"

11:57) But the Chief Priests and the Pharisees had given orders that if anyone knew where Jesus was, they were to report it, so they could arrest him.

---

[225] The third and final Passover mentioned in the Gospel.

Chapter 12

12:1) Six days before the Passover, Jesus arrived at Bethany. (This is where Lazaros lived, the same one who had died, and whom Jesus had raised from the dead.) 12:2) A dinner was prepared for Jesus; Martha attended to all the preparations, and Lazaros was among those who reclined at table with him. 12:3) Mary took a liter[226] of very costly myrrh, genuine oil of spikenard, and anointed the feet of Jesus, gently wiping his feet dry with her hair. And the house was perfumed, filled with the fragrance of the myrrh.

12:4) One of his disciples, Judas Iscariot (the son of Simon – the one who was about to betray him), feigned, 12:5) "Why was this myrrh not sold for three hundred denarii and given to the poor?" 12:6) (He did not say this because he cared for the poor, but because he was a thief. He even had charge of the moneybox and used to steal its contents.)

12:7) "Leave her be," Jesus replied. "She has been saving this for the day of my burial. 12:8) You will always have the poor, but you will not always have me."

---

[226] A Greek liter had a liquid measurement of around 8.5 fluid ounces.

12:9) A large crowd of Judeans[227] had learned that Jesus was there, and they came not only for Jesus, but also to see Lazaros, whom Jesus had raised from the dead. 12:10) The Chief Priests were already plotting to kill Lazaros as well. 12:11) Because of him, many Judeans[228] were flocking to Jesus and putting their faith in him.

12:12) On the next day, the great rush of people who had come for the Passover heard that Jesus was on his way to Jerusalem. 12:13) They cut branches from palm trees and went out to meet him, shouting "Hosanna!"[229]

"Blessed is he who comes in the name of the Lord![230]

"The King of Israel!"

12:14) Jesus found a young foal and seated himself on it. As it is written, 12:15) "Fear not, Daughter of Sion! Behold, your King is coming, seated upon the foal of a burro."[231] 12:16) (At first, his disciples did not fully understand these things, but after Jesus was glorified, they remembered that he had accomplished the

---

[227] Greek, *Ioudaios.*
[228] *Ibid.*
[229] Psalm 118:25, a liturgical exclamation in Hebrew or Aramaic, originally meaning "Help" or "Save."
[230] Psalm 118:26.
[231] Zechariah 9:9.

very things that were written in the Scriptures concerning him.) 12:17) The people of the crowd, those who had been with Jesus when he called Lazaros from the tomb and raised him from the dead, confirmed what had happened. 12:18) This was the reason that the Passover crowds went out to meet him, because they had heard that Jesus had performed this sign.

12:19) But the Pharisees grumbled to each other: "Can't you see?"

"Nothing does any good."

"Look! The whole world has gone after him!"

12:20) Some Greeks who had come to worship at the Feast 12:21) approached Philip (the one from Bethsaïda in Galilee). "Sir," they asked him, "we want to see Jesus." 12:22) Philip went to Andrew and told him, and Andrew and Philip together related the request to Jesus.

12:23) Jesus responded to them, "The hour has come for the Son of Man to be glorified. 12:24) Amen, amen, I say to you, unless a grain of wheat falls into the ground and dies, it remains alone. But if it does die, it brings forth an abundant harvest. 12:25) If you cling to your existence, you will lose it, but if you can hate your existence in this world, you will preserve yourself for eternal life. 12:26) All who would serve me must follow me. And where I am, there will my servant be also. And all who would serve me, Love will honor them. 12:27) Now, my soul is shaken to the core, and what am I to say: 'Love, save me from this hour?' But this is the reason I have come to this hour. 12:28) Love! Glorify your name!"

"I have indeed glorified it!" a voice thundered from heaven, "and I shall glorify it again!"

12:29) Some in the crowd standing there who heard the voice shouted, "Was that thunder?"

Others insisted, "No, it was an angel that spoke to him!"

12:30) "This voice did not happen for me," Jesus told them, "but for you. 12:31) Now is the judgment of this world. Now is the despot[232] of this world cast out. 12:32) And I, if I be exalted from the earth, I shall draw all people to myself." 12:33) (Jesus said this to signify the manner of death he was to die.)

12:34) The crowd called back to him: "We have heard in the Law that the Messiah abides forever."[233]

---

[232] Greek, *archon.*
[233] Isaiah 9:7; Ezekiel 37:25.

"So how do you say the Son of Man must be lifted up?"

"Who is this Son of Man?"

12:35) "Just a little while longer and the light is with you," Jesus exhorted them. "Walk while you have the light, so the darkness may not overwhelm you. People who walk in darkness do not know where they are going. 12:36) While you have the light, trust in the light, that you may become children of light." When Jesus finished speaking, he departed and hid from them.

12:37) With all the signs that Jesus worked in front of their eyes, still they did not trust in him. 12:38) This was so the saying of the Prophet Isaiah might be fulfilled, which states, "O Love, who has believed our account? And to whom has the mighty arm of Love been revealed?"[234] 12:39) This is why they were unable to come to faith, because, as Isaiah says again, 12:40) "I have blinded their eyes and hardened their hearts, lest they see with their eyes and perceive in their hearts and turn back, and I heal them."[235] 12:41) Isaiah said these things when he beheld his glory and spoke concerning him.[236] 12:42) Yet many of the leadership did believe in Jesus. However, they kept silent in public on account of the

---

[234] Isaiah 53:1, LXX (adapted).
[235] Isaiah 6:9,10.
[236] See Isaiah 6.

Pharisees, who would expel them from the synagogue. 12:43) For they held dear the glory of others, rather than the glory of Love.

12:44) But Jesus lifted up his voice and cried aloud, "If you believe in me, you do not merely believe in me, but in Love that sent me! 12:45) And if you have seen me, you have seen the one that sent me. 12:46) I have come – light for the world – that everyone who believes in me might not remain in darkness. 12:47) Indeed, all who hear my words and do not believe, I do not judge them. Truly, I have not come to judge the world, but to heal the world. 12:48) If you break faith with me and reject my words, you have your judge – the Message that I have spoken – that Message shall judge you on the Final Day. 12:49) For I have not spoken of myself. Rather it is Love that sent me. Love laid the commandment on me, what I was to say and what I was to speak. 12:50) Indeed, I know the commandment of Love is eternal life. Therefore, what I say, I say it as Love declared it to me."

Chapter 13

13:1) Just before the Feast of the Passover, Jesus acknowledged that the moment for him to pass over from this world to Love had finally come. Jesus loved those who were his own in the world and he showed them the perfection of his love.

13:2) When the supper was finished, (the devil having already put into the heart of Judas Iscariot, the son of Simon, to betray him), 13:3) Jesus, with full awareness that Love had delivered everything into his hands, and that he had come from Love and was going to Love, 13:4) arose from the supper and set aside his garments. Then he took a towel and girded himself. 13:5) Next, he filled a basin with water and commenced washing the feet of his disciples, wiping them dry with the towel that was wrapped around his waist. 13:6) Then, Jesus approached Simon Peter.

Peter protested. "You Lord? You are going to wash my feet?"

13:7) "What I am doing now," Jesus said to him, "you do not understand. But later on, you will come to know its meaning for yourself."

13:8) "You shall never, ever wash my feet!" Peter insisted.

"If I do not wash you," Jesus reassured him, "you have no destiny with me."

13:9) "Lord, not only my feet," Simon Peter exclaimed to him, "but my hands and head as well!"

13:10) Jesus said to him, "Someone who has just come from the bath has no need to wash except for their feet, rather, they are clean through and through. Indeed, you are clean, but not all of you." 13:11) For Jesus knew the identity of his betrayer – (that is why he said, 'Not all of you are clean'). 13:12) When Jesus had finished washing their feet, he put his garments back on and reclined again with them at supper.

"Do you realize what I have done for you?" Jesus asked them. 13:13) "You call me 'Teacher' and 'Lord' and you say rightly for so I am. 13:14) Therefore if I, your Lord and Teacher, have washed your feet, should you not also wash one another's feet? 13:15) Truly, I have given you an example, that just as I have done for you, you should do for one another as well. 13:16) Amen, amen, I say to you, no slave is greater than his master; nor are apostles, the ones sent, greater than the one who sends them.

13:17) If you understand these things, happy and blessed are you if you act on them.

13:18) "I do not speak about all of you. I know whom I have chosen for myself, but this is for the fulfillment of the Scripture, 'He who eats the bread with me has his raised heel against me'.[237] 13:19) I am telling you this now – before it happens – so that when it does happen you will believe that I Am.[238] 13:20) Amen, amen, I say to you, if you receive the one I send, you receive me, and when you receive me, you receive the one who sent me." 13:21) After he said this, Jesus became agitated and troubled in spirit. He bore it witness saying, "Amen, amen, I say to you, one of you will betray me!"

13:22) The disciples began to glance around at each other, at a loss about whom he was speaking. 13:23) One of his disciples, a bosom friend of Jesus whom he dearly loved,[239] was reclining at the supper close by Jesus' side. 13:24) Simon Peter motioned to him to see if he could learn about whom Jesus was speaking.

---

[237] Psalm 41:9, the original in both the Hebrew and the Septuagint reads "of my bread."

[238] See note 111.

[239] John the Evangelist himself, the son of Zebedee and Salome, who, by Orthodox Christian tradition, was one of the two daughters of Joseph. Thus John was a nephew of Jesus by marriage. See footnote 89.

13:25) That disciple leaned back on Jesus' chest and asked him, "Lord, who is it?"

13:26) Jesus answered, "It is the one to whom I will hand the morsel of bread I am dipping." And Jesus dipped the morsel of bread, and gave it to Judas Iscariot, the son of Simon. 13:27) After he partook of the morsel, Satan entered him. Jesus spoke to Judas "What you do, do quickly."

13:28) No one at the supper understood the meaning of what Jesus said to him. 13:29) Some of them thought that Jesus had told him, 'Go buy some items needed for the Feast,' or that he should give something to the poor, inasmuch as Judas held the moneybox. 13:30) Once Judas had taken the morsel, he left straightaway. And it was night.

13:31) After he left, Jesus continued, "Now is the Son of Man glorified. And Love is glorified in him. 13:32) If Love is glorified in him, not only will Love glorify him within Herself; Love will glorify him at this very instant. 13:33) O little children, I am with you only a little while. You will seek me, and as I said to the Judeans,[240] 'Where I am going, you cannot come'[241] – now I say it also to you.

13:34) "A new commandment I give to you, that you love one another – that you love one another as I have loved you. 13:35) This is how all people will know that you are my followers, if you love one another."

13:36) "Lord, where are you going?" Simon Peter asked him.

"Where I am going, you cannot follow me just yet," Jesus answered him, "but later, you *will* follow me."[242]

13:37) "Lord, why can I not follow you right now?" Peter pressed him. "I will sacrifice my life for you!"[243]

13:38) "You would sacrifice your life for me?" Jesus replied to him. "Amen, amen, I say to you, the cock will not crow before you will deny me thrice!"

---

[240] Greek, *Ioudaios*.

[241] John 8:21.

[242] According to tradition, Peter was martyred for Jesus at Rome during the reign of Nero. He was crucified on the Vatican Hill upside down at his own request, so as not to imitate his Lord.

[243] See footnote 194; and so in the next verse.

Chapter 14[244]

14:1) "Let not your heart be troubled. Do you believe in Love? Believe also in me. 14:2) In the house of Love are many mansions.[245] If it were not so, I would have told you. I am crossing over in order to prepare a place for you, 14:3) and if I go and prepare a place for you, I will come again and take you to myself, so that where I am, you may also be. 14:4) You know where I am going. You also know the way."

14:5) "Lord," Thomas implored him, "how can we know the way when we do not know where you are going?"

14:6) "I Am[246] the way, and the truth, and the life," Jesus said to him. "No one comes to Love except through me. 14:7) If you had known me, you would have also known Love; and from this very moment, you both know and see Love."

14:8) "Lord, show us Love," Philip said to him, "and we will be satisfied."

14:9) "So much time am I with you, Philip," Jesus comforted him, "and still you do not recognize me? Those who

---

[244] This dialogue of Jesus with his disciples continues through chapter 16.

[245] In the New Testament, the Greek word *mone* occurs only in this verse and verse 14:23, where it is translated "cloister." It is the origin of the word "monastery," the place where one dwells alone with God.

[246] See note 111.

have seen me have seen Love; so how can you say, 'show us Love'?[247] 14:10) Do you not believe that I am inside Love and Love is inside me? The words that I speak to you, I do not speak of myself. It is Love that dwells in me; Love accomplishes the works. 14:11) Trust me, I am within Love and Love is within me. If not, then believe me for the sake of these deeds. 14:12) Amen, amen, I say to you, those who believe in me – the deeds that I accomplish – they shall also do them and even greater ones, because I am going to Love. 14:13) Whatever you ask in my name, I will do it, that Love may be glorified in the Son. 14:14) If you request something in my name, I *will* do it.

14:15) "If you love me, keep my commandments. 14:16) and I will ask Love to give you still another Advocate – the Paraclete – to abide with you forever, 14:17) the Spirit of truth. The world cannot receive the Spirit, because it neither sees nor recognizes it. But you know the Spirit because it abides with you and is within you. 14:18) I will not leave you orphans; I will come to you. 14:19) Yet a little while and the world sees me no more, but you will see me; because I live, you will live also. 14:20) On

---

[247] Compare with the Buddha to his follower, Vakkali: "Whoever sees the Dharma sees me; whoever sees me sees the Dharma. Truly seeing Dharma, one sees me; seeing me, one sees Dharma." (*Samyutta Nikaya*, 22.87)

That Day,[248] you will know that I am in Love, and that you are in me, and that I am in you. 14:21) You who hold fast to my commandments and keep them, you are the ones who love me. And you who love me shall be cherished by Love, and I shall love you and reveal myself to you."

14:22) Judas[249] (not the "Iscariot") asked him, "Lord, and what is going to happen that you will reveal yourself to us, but not to the world?"

14:23) Jesus responded, "If you love me, you will keep my word, and Love will cherish you and we will come to you and create a cloister[250] within you. Those who do not keep my words do not love me. 14:24) And the Message that you are hearing is not my own; it is of Love that sent me. 14:25) I have spoken these things to you while I yet remain with you. 14:26) But the Paraclete, the Holy Spirit that Love will send in my name, will be your teacher in all things, and bring to your remembrance everything I have told you.

---

[248] The Day of Resurrection.
[249] Or "Judah," the son of Iakovos, mentioned in Luke 6:16. In the Gospels of Matthew and Mark, he is called Levvaios and Thaddeus, respectively.
[250] See note 245.

14:27) "Peace I leave you. My own peace I give you; not as the world gives do I give to you. Let not your heart be troubled, neither let it be afraid. 14:28) You heard me tell you that I am going away and I am coming to you. If you loved me, you would be glad that I said I was going to Love, because Love is greater than I. 14:29) And now I have declared it to you before it happens, so that when it does happen, you may believe. 14:30) I will no longer say much to you, for the despot[251] of this world is coming, and he has nothing over me. 14:31) But so that the world may know that I cherish Love – indeed just as Love has commanded me – so shall I do. Arise! Let us go forth!"

---

[251] See note 232.

Chapter 15[252]

15:1) "I Am[253] the true vine and Love is the vinedresser. 15:2) Love removes every branch in me that bears no fruit. But Love prunes and purges every branch that does bear fruit, so that it may bring forth even more fruit. 15:3) Now you are already purified on account of the Message[254] I have spoken to you. 15:4) Abide in me, as I abide in you. Just as the branch cannot bear fruit of itself unless it remains in the vine, neither can you unless you abide in me.

15:5) "I Am[255] the vine; you are the branches. Abide in me as I abide in you and you will yield abundant fruit, because you cannot accomplish anything without me. 15:6) Those who do not remain in me will be tossed outside like a branch and wither; others will gather them up, throw them into the fire, and they will be burned.

15:7) "If you abide in me and my sayings[256] abide in you, ask for whatever you desire, and it shall come to pass for you.

---

[252] Jesus may be speaking as they pass by vineyards, walking from the Upper Room, the site of the Supper, to the Garden of Gethsemane.
[253] See note 111.
[254] Greek, *logos.*
[255] See note 111.
[256] Greek, *rhema.*

15:8) By this is Love glorified, that you bear abundant fruit, and so you will become my disciples. 15:9) Just as Love has cherished me, even so have I loved you. Abide in my love. 15:10) If you keep my commandments, you will abide in my love, even as I kept the commandments of Love and abide in Her love. 15:11) I have spoken these things to you so that my joy may abide in you, and so that your joy may be complete.

15:12) "This is my commandment: Love one another as I have loved you. 15:13) You can have no greater love than this, to sacrifice[257] your life for your friends. 15:14) If you do all that I command, then you are my friends. 15:15) I call you servants no more, for a servant does not know what his lord is doing. But I proclaim you my friends, because all that I heard from Love I have made known to you. 15:16) You have not chosen me, but I have chosen you. Moreover, I have ordained[258] you to go forth and bear fruit. And your fruit shall endure, so that whatever you ask of Love in my name, She will give it to you. 15:17) Love one another; this is my commandment to you.

---

[257] See note 194.
[258] Greek, *tithemi.*

90

15:18) "If the world hates you, know that it hated me first. 15:19) If you were of the world, the world would love its own. There is a reason the world hates you; because you are not of the world. I have chosen you for myself out of the world. 15:20) Remember the saying I told you, 'no slave is greater than his master.'[259] If they persecuted me, they will persecute you. If they keep my word, they will keep yours also. 15:21) Nevertheless, they will do all manner of things to you on account of my name, because they have not known the one who sent me. 15:22) If I had not come and spoken to them, they would have no fault. But now they have no excuse for their error. 15:23) Those who hate me also hate Love. 15:24) If I had not accomplished the deeds among them that no other person has ever done, they would have no fault. But now they have not only seen, but they have hated both me and Love. 15:25) All this so the saying written in their own Law might be fulfilled, 'They hated me without cause.'[260]

15:26) "Now when the Paraclete comes, which I shall send to you from Love – the Spirit of truth that proceeds from Love – it

---

[259] 13:16.
[260] Psalm 35:19, 69:4.

will bear witness concerning me, 15:27) and you also will bear witness, because you were with me from the beginning."

Chapter 16[261]

16:1) "I have said these things to you so you will not be scandalized. 16:2) They are going to expel you from the assemblies. A time is coming when anyone who puts you to death will think they are doing God a religious service. 16:3) They will do these things because they know neither Love nor me. 16:4) But I have told you about this so that when the time comes, you can remember that I *did* tell you. At the beginning, I did not say these things to you, because I was with you.

16:5) "And now, I am going to the one who sent me. Yet, none of you asks me, 'Where are you going?' 16:6) Rather, because I have said these things to you, sadness has filled your hearts. 16:7) But it is to your good that I leave. I am telling you the truth. If I do not go, the Comforter will not come to you. But if I cross over, I will send the Comforter to you. 16:8) The Comforter will come and expose the truth about the world: concerning error, righteousness, and judgment. 16:9) Concerning error, because they do not believe in me; 16:10) concerning righteousness, because I

---

[261] The chapter break does not indicate a break in scene.

am going to Love and you will see me no more; 16:11) concerning judgment, because the tyrant[262] of this world is judged!

16:12) "I have so much more to tell you, but you cannot bear it now. 16:13) But the Spirit of truth will come and guide you into all truth. For the Spirit will not speak of itself, but will relate what it hears, and will declare to you the things that are to come. 16:14) The Spirit will glorify me, because it will receive from mine and declare it to you. 16:15) Everything that Love has is mine. This is why I said 'It will receive from mine and declare it to you.' 16:16) A little while and you will not see me, and again a little while, and you will see me."

16:17) His disciples began to ask among themselves: "What is he saying to us?"

"'A little while and you will not see me'..."

"'and again a little while, and you will see me?'"

"And 'I am going to Love'?"

16:18) "What is this 'little while' he is talking about?"

"We don't know what he is talking about!"

---

[262] See note 232.

16:19) Jesus knew what they wanted to ask him and said to them, "Is this what you seek to find the meaning of among yourselves – what I said, 'A little while and you will not see me, and again a little while, and you will see me?'[263] 16:20) Amen, amen, I say to you, you will weep and mourn, but the world will rejoice! Yes, you will be overcome by sorrow, but your sorrow will give birth[264] to joy. 16:21) When a woman is in labor,[265] she has pain because her time has come. But when she has brought forth the child, she no longer remembers her distress because of her joy that a human being[266] is born into the world.

16:22) "So now, sorrow has seized you, but I will see you again and your hearts will rejoice, and no one will take your joy from you! 16:23) Indeed, on That Day,[267] you will not ask anything of me. Amen, amen, I say to you, whatever you ask of Love in my name, She will grant it to you. 16:24) Till now, you have not requested anything in my name. Ask! And you will receive, that your joy may be complete!

---

[263] 16:17.

[264] Greek, *gignomai.*

[265] Greek, *tikto.*

[266] Greek, *anthropos.*

[267] See footnote 248.

16:25) "I have spoken to you about these things with metaphors,[268] but the time is coming when I will no longer speak to you in symbols,[269] but I will tell you about Love plainly and directly. 16:26) On That Day, you will make requests in my name – and I do not say that I shall ask Love for you – 16:27) for Love cherishes and loves you, because you have loved me and have believed that I came forth from Love. 16:28) I came forth from Love and came to the world. Now I am letting go of the world and going back to Love."

16:29) His disciples replied to him, "See, now you are speaking directly and not reciting some proverb!"

16:30) "Now we realize that you know everything."

"And you have no need to be questioned by anybody."

"This is why we believe that you came forth from Love."

16:31) "Now you finally believe?" Jesus exclaimed. 16:32) "Behold, the hour is coming and has now arrived for you to be scattered, each to his own, and to leave me alone. Yet, I am not alone, because Love is with me. 16:33) I have told you these things

---

[268] Greek, *paroimia*; translated as "proverb" in 16:29.
[269] *Ibid.*

so that in me you might have peace. In the world, you will have

tribulation; but have courage! I have conquered the world!"

Chapter 17

17:1) Jesus concluded these words, lifted his eyes heavenward, and said, "Love, the hour has come. Glorify your Son, that your Son may glorify you, 17:2) even as you have given him authority over every sentient being[270] to grant eternal life to all whom you have entrusted to him. 17:3) And this is eternal life – to know you, the only true Love, and to know the one whom you have sent, Jesus Christ.

17:4) "I glorified you upon earth. I completed the work that you gave me to accomplish. 17:5) And now, O Love, at this moment, glorify me with the glory that is yours, the glory that I had with you before there was a world!

17:6) "I revealed your name to the men and women who were your gift to me from the world. They belonged to you and you gave them to me, and they have upheld your Message.[271] 17:7) Now they understand that everything that you have given to me *is* from you, 17:8) because the words[272] that you gave to me, I gave to them, and they accepted these words. Truly, they realize that I came forth from you; they believe that you sent me. 17:9) I make

---

[270] Greek, *sarx.*
[271] Greek, *logos.*
[272] Greek, *rhema.*

this request for them; I do not ask for the world. Rather, I ask for those you have entrusted to me, for they are yours. 17:10) All that is mine is yours and all that is yours is mine, and I am glorified in them. 17:11) But I am no longer in the world. They are in the world, and I am coming to you.

"O Holy Love, watch over them by your name, the name you have given to me, so that they may be one, even as we are. 17:12) When I was with them in the world, I watched over them by your name. I protected those you entrusted to me, and not one of them was lost, save the lost son, that the Scripture might be fulfilled.[273]

17:13) "But now I am coming to you, and I speak these things in the world that they may possess my joy overflowing within them. 17:14) I gave them your Message, and the world hated them because they are not of the world, even as I am not of the world. 17:15) I do not ask you to take them out of the world, rather I ask you to protect them from the evil one. 17:16) They are not of the world, just as I am not of the world.

---

[273] Cf. Psalm 109:8

17:17) "Sanctify them by your truth. Your Word is truth.[274]

17:18) As you sent me into the world, even so I have sent them into the world. 17:19) And for their sakes I sanctify myself, that they also might be sanctified by the truth. 17:20) And I ask not only for these, but also for those who believe in me because of them; 17:21) that they may be one, even as you, Love, are in me and I am in you, that they may also be one in us, that the world might believe that you sent me. 17:22) And the glory that you gave to me, I have given to them, that they might be one, even as we are one; 17:23) I in them and you in me, that they might be perfected in one, so that the world might know that you have sent me, and that you love them even as you love me.

17:24) "O Love, for those you have entrusted to me, I dearly want them to be with me where I am, to behold my glory – the glory that you gave me, because you loved me before the foundation of the cosmos. 17:25) O righteous Love, the world does not know you, but I know you and they know that you sent me. 17:26) I did indeed make your name known to them, and I shall

---

[274] Greek, *O Logos o sos aletheia estin.*

make it known again, so that the love with which you loved me may be in them, even as I am in them."

Chapter 18

18:1) When Jesus finished speaking, he moved on with his disciples to the other side of the Kidron Wadi,[275] where there was a garden. Jesus entered the garden with his disciples. 18:2) Judas, who betrayed him, was familiar with the place, because Jesus would often gather there with his disciples. 18:3) Judas massed a company of garrison soldiers[276] and some of the subordinates of the Chief Priests and Pharisees, and went there with torches, lanterns, and weapons.

18:4) Jesus, because he knew everything that was to come upon him, stepped forward and said, "Whom do you seek?"

18:5) "Jesus the Nazarene!"[277] they shouted back at him.

"I Am,"[278] Jesus told them.

Judas, the one who betrayed him, was standing with the soldiers. 18:6) As soon as[279] Jesus answered them, "I Am,"[280] they were all thrust backwards and fell to the ground.

18:7) "Whom do you seek?" Jesus asked them again.

---

[275] A dried up watercourse to the east of Jerusalem, which runs to the Dead Sea.
[276] Greek, *speira,* a Roman cohort, indicating these were Roman soldiers, put at the disposal of the Temple authorities.
[277] Greek, *Nazoraios.*
[278] See note 111.
[279] See Appendix I.
[280] See note 111.

"Jesus the Nazarene!" they fulminated.

18:8) "I told you that I Am,"[281] Jesus replied, "so if you are looking for me, let these men go." 18:9) (That the word that he spoke might be fulfilled, 'I lost not one of those whom you entrusted to me.'[282])

18:10) Then Simon Peter drew his short-sword and struck the slave of the High Priest, slicing through his right ear. The slave's name was Malchos.[283]

18:11) "Put your sword back in its sheath!" Jesus ordered Peter. "The cup that Love has given to me, am I never to drink it?"

18:12) The garrison commander, the soldiers, and the subordinates of the religious authorities[284] placed Jesus under arrest. They bound him 18:13) and dragged him away. First, they went to Annas,[285] the father-in-law of Caiaphas, the High Priest for the cycle of that year. 18:14) Caiaphas was the one who had

---

[281] *Ibid.*

[282] 17:12.

[283] Luke adds the detail that Jesus touched Malchos' ear and healed him (Luke 22:51).

[284] Greek, *Ioudaios*.

[285] Annas was High Priest from 6 – 15 AD.

advised the leadership[286] that it was expedient for one man to perish for the people.[287]

18:15) Peter and the Other Disciple[288] followed Jesus. This particular disciple was acquainted with the High Priest[289] and entered the courtyard of the High Priest at the same time as Jesus. 18:16) Peter, on the other hand, stood outside by the door. So, the Other Disciple (the one acquainted with the High Priest) went out, spoke to the gatekeeper, and brought Peter inside.

18:17) The gatekeeper, a young serving girl, queried Peter, "Aren't you also one of this man's followers?"

"No, I'm not!" Peter snapped.

18:18) Some of the slaves and other servants who had been milling about built a fire because the weather was cold. They warmed themselves by the fire, and Peter stood right along side them, warming himself.

18:19) All this time, the High Priest was interrogating Jesus, questioning him about his students and his teaching.

---

[286] Greek, *Ioudaios*.
[287] Cf. 11:49,50.
[288] John the Evangelist.
[289] Annas, and so through verse 24.

18:20) "I have spoken openly to the world," Jesus replied to him. "My teaching has always been in the synagogue and in the Temple, where believers[290] are wont to gather. I said nothing in secret. 18:21) Why are you asking me? Ask those who heard what I said to them. You will see; they know what I said."

18:22) But when Jesus said this, one of the henchmen who was restraining him slapped him across the mouth, barking, "Is that how you talk to the High Priest?"

18:23) Jesus turned to him, "If I spoke dishonestly, then show some evidence of the dishonesty, but if honestly, why did you hit me?" 18:24) Then Annas sent him off to Caiaphas the High Priest, bound hand and foot.

18:25) All the while, Peter had been standing around and warming himself by the fire, when someone said to him, "Aren't you also one of his followers?"

18:26) He denied it, "I am not!"

But a slave of the High Priest, a relative of the man whose ear Peter had severed, demanded, "Didn't I see you in the garden

---

[290] Greek, *Ioudaios*.

with him?" 18:27) And Peter denied it yet again, and at once the cock crowed.

18:28) Later, they[291] marched Jesus from Caiaphas to the Praetorium. Morning had broken. But they would not enter the Praetorium because they wanted to partake of the Passover meal, and to go inside would have ritually defiled them.

18:29) Consequently, Pilate had to go outside to meet with them. "What accusation do you bring against this man?" he demanded.

18:30) "If this man were not a criminal," they answered him, "we would not have turned him over to you."

18:31) "Then take him yourselves and judge him according to your own law." Pilate came back at them.

"It is not lawful for us to put anyone to death," they[292] protested. 18:32) (That the saying[293] of Jesus might be fulfilled, which he spoke concerning the way he was about to be put to

---

[291] The group was composed of some of the Chief Priests (see vs. 35), their subordinates and perhaps some Pharisees.
[292] Greek, *Ioudaios*.
[293] Greek, *logos*.

death.)[294] 18:33) Then Pilate went back into the Praetorium and called for Jesus.

"Are you the king of the Jews?" he demanded of him.

18:34) "Are you saying this of yourself," Jesus replied to him, "or did others tell you this about me?"

18:35) "What! Am I a Jew?" Pilate retorted. "Your own people and Chief Priests turned you over to me. What did you do?"

18:36) "My kingdom is not of this world," Jesus answered. "If my kingdom were of this world, my subjects would have put up a fight in order to keep them[295] from taking me. But for now, my kingdom is not of this place."

18:37) "Aha!" Pilate snapped at him, "then you are a king!"

"You say that I am a king," Jesus replied. "I was born for this – I came into the world for this – to bear witness to the truth. All who are of the truth listen to my voice."

18:38) "What is truth?" jested Pilate.[296] After he said this, he went out again to the crowd.[297] He told them, "I don't find anything criminal in him, 18:39) but you have a custom that I set

---

[294] Cf. 3:14, 12:32.

[295] Greek, *Ioudaios*.

[296] After Sir Francis Bacon (The Essays): "'What is truth?' said jesting Pilate, and would not stay for an answer."

[297] Greek, *Ioudaios*.

someone free during the Passover. Now then, do you want me to set free the king of the Jews?"

"Not him!" they all shouted back. They yelled out instead, "Barabbas!" (This Barabbas was an outlaw.)

Chapter 19

19:1) Then Pilate took Jesus and had him flogged. 19:2) The soldiers plaited a crown of thorns and rammed it on his head. They also draped him with a purple cloak 19:3) and jeered, "All hail the king of the Jews!" And they kept slapping him across his face.

19:4) Pilate went back outside and addressed the crowd, "Look, I am going to bring him out to you, so you can be certain that I find absolutely nothing criminal in him." 19:5) Then Jesus emerged, wearing the crown of thorns and the purple robe. "Behold! The Man!" Pilate taunted the crowd.

19:6) When the Chief Priests and their subordinates saw Jesus, they began shouting, "Crucify! Crucify him!"

"Take him yourselves and crucify him!" Pilate sneered at them. "Frankly, I find no fault in him."

19:7) "We have a law!" the leaders[298] called out.

"And according to our law he should be put to death!"

"Because he made himself out to be the Son of God!"

---

[298] Greek, *Ioudaios*.

19:8) When Pilate heard this, he became more nervous. 19:9) He went back inside the Praetorium and demanded of Jesus, "Where did you come from?" But Jesus gave him no reply. 19:10) "You will not speak to me? Do you not understand that I have the power to crucify you and the power to release you?"

19:11) Jesus responded, "You would have no authority over me unless it was granted to you from on high. That is why those who handed me over to you bear the greater guilt."

19:12) As a result of this exchange, Pilate began looking for a way to release Jesus. But the leadership[299] hectored him, "If you release him, you are no friend of Caesar!"

"Anyone who makes himself a king declares himself against Caesar!"

19:13) When Pilate heard this, he had Jesus dragged outside. Then, he took his seat on the Tribunal[300] in the place that is called *Lithostrotos*[301] (in Hebrew, *Gabbatha*). 19:14) It was Friday, the Day of Preparation for the Passover, around the sixth hour.[302]

---

[299] Greek, *Ioudaios*.
[300] The Judgment Seat.
[301] "Laid with stones" or "Pavement."
[302] Noon, the hour when the ritual slaughter of the Passover lambs commenced.

110

"Look! Your king!" he provoked the crowd.[303]

19:15) They clamored "Off with him!"

"Off with him!"

"Crucify him!"

Pilate scoffed at them, "Shall I crucify your king?"

"We have no king but Caesar!" the Chief Priests shouted.

19:16) And that was the moment when he turned Jesus over to them[304] for crucifixion. They grabbed hold of Jesus and dragged him away. 19:17) Bearing his cross, Jesus went forth to the place called "The Place of the Skull" (it is called *Golgotha* in Hebrew). *The soldiers gave him a mixture of vinegary wine and pain-killing wormwood to drink, but when he tasted it, he would not drink it.[305] 19:18) There they crucified him, and two others with him on either side, with Jesus in the middle. *And Jesus said, "Love, forgive them, for they know not what they do."[306]

19:19) Pilate had a placard lettered and posted on top of the cross. And this is what was written, "Jesus the Nazarene: The King

---

[303] Greek, *Ioudaios*.

[304] This word, *autos* in Greek, seems to point to the Chief Priests, but in acceding to the demand for Jesus' crucifixion, Pilate turns Jesus over to his own Roman soldiers to carry out the sentence, as evidenced by 19:23.

[305] Matthew 27:34. As the destroyer of death by his own death, Jesus does not shrink from experiencing and transmuting the fullness of suffering.

[306] Luke 23:34, adapted.

of the Jews." 19:20) The place where Jesus was crucified was right outside the City and consequently, many people[307] read the placard, which was written in Hebrew, Greek, and Latin.

19:21) The Chief Priests[308] complained to Pilate, "Do not write, 'The King of the Jews,' but rather, 'This man said, I am King of the Jews'."

19:22) Pilate answered, "I wrote what I wrote."

19:23) After they had crucified Jesus, the soldiers took his garments and made of them four piles, a share for each soldier, as well as the robe. However, the robe was seamless, woven from the top all the way through. 19:24) "Don't rip it," one of them said. "Let's draw lots to see who gets it." (That the Scripture be fulfilled which said, "They divided my garments among themselves and over my robe they cast lots.")[309]

While the soldiers were doing this, 19:25) his Mother, his Mother's sister, Maria the wife of Clopas, and Mary Magdalene were standing by the cross of Jesus. 19:26) Jesus looked at his Mother and the disciple[310] whom he loved standing next to her.

---

[307] Greek, *Ioudaios*.

[308] Text adds "of the Jews," (Greek, *Ioudaios*), omitted here as redundant.

[309] Psalm 22:18, (21:19 LXX).

[310] John the Evangelist.

112

Jesus said to his Mother, "My Lady, behold your son!" 19:27)
Then he said to the disciple, "Behold your mother!" And from that
very moment, the disciple took her to his home.

*Those who passed by cursed Jesus, wagging their heads
and saying, "You would tear down the temple and rebuild it in
three days?"

"Save yourself!"

"If you are God's Son, come down from the cross!"

The Chief Priests also mocked him, along with the Scribes,
the Elders, and the Pharisees, saying, "He saved others, but he
cannot save himself!"

"If he is the king of Israel, let him come down now from
the cross and we will believe him."

"He trusted in God, let him deliver him, if he wants him,
for he said 'I am the Son of God'."[311]

*Then one of the outlaws hanging on the gibbet cursed at
him, saying, "Aren't you the Messiah? Save yourself and us too!"

But the other one rebuked him, saying, "Don't you fear
God? You're under the same sentence! And justly so for us; we're

---

[311] Matthew 27:39-43.

getting what we deserve. But this man did nothing wrong." Then he said to Jesus, "Remember me, Lord, when you come into your kingdom."

And Jesus said to him, "Amen I tell you, today you will be with me in paradise."[312]

*Now from the sixth hour there was darkness over all the land until the ninth hour. At the ninth hour Jesus cried out with a loud voice, *"Eloï! Eloï! lama sabachthani?"*[313] which translates, "My God! My God! Why have you abandoned me?" When some of the people standing there heard this, they said, "Look, he's calling for Elias."[314]

19:28) After this, Jesus, knowing that he had completed everything, said "I thirst," (that the Scripture might be fulfilled).[315] 19:29) There was a jar full of vinegar sitting there, and someone soaked a sponge with it, put it on a stalk of hyssop, and held it up to his mouth. 19:30a) When Jesus had taken the vinegar, he uttered, "Consummation."[316] *Then he called out with a loud voice

---

[312] Luke 23:39-43.
[313] Aramaic for Psalm 22:1.
[314] Mark 15:33-35.
[315] Cf. Psalm 69:21.
[316] The Greek, *tetelestai,* is a single word that is literally translated "It has been consummated," or "It is consummated."

and said, "Love! Into your hands I entrust my spirit!"[317] 19:30b) And when he had bowed his head, he yielded up his breath of life.[318]

19:31) Because it was the Day of Preparation,[319] the religious authorities[320] asked Pilate to have their legs broken[321] and their bodies removed. This was so that they would not remain on the cross during the Sabbath, because that particular Sabbath day was most important.[322]

19:32) So the soldiers went and broke the legs of the first man, and then those of the other man who was crucified with Jesus. 19:33) But when they came to Jesus and saw that he was already dead, they did not break his legs. 19:34) Rather, one of the soldiers stabbed his side with a lance and there was an instant outpouring of blood and water. 19:35) Indeed, he[323] who saw it gives his testimony, and his testimony is truthful, and he knows that he speaks the truth so that you may also believe. 19:36) For

---

[317] Luke 23:46 (adapted).

[318] By bowing his head *before* expiring, Jesus shows that, as the conqueror of death, he commands death to come.

[319] Friday.

[320] Greek, *Ioudaios*.

[321] So the victim would collapse and asphyxiate as soon as possible.

[322] The Passover itself.

[323] John the Evangelist, who has returned to the site of the Crucifixion after removing the Virgin Mary (19:27).

these things happened that the Scripture might be fulfilled, "Not a bone of his was broken."[324] 19:37) And again another Scripture says, "They shall look on him whom they have pierced."[325]

19:38) Later on, Joseph of Arimathaia (a follower of Jesus – although a secret one, because he was afraid of the religious authorities[326]) begged Pilate that he might retrieve the body of Jesus. And Pilate gave his permission. Then Joseph went and recovered the body of Jesus. 19:39) Nikodemos, who had first come to Jesus at night, went along as well, bringing one hundred liters[327] of a mixture of myrrh and aloe. 19:40) They took the body of Jesus and wrapped it in grave-linens[328] with the aromatic spices, as is customary in Jewish burials.

19:41) Now there was a garden in the place where Jesus was crucified, and in the garden a new tomb in which no one had ever been buried.[329] 19:42) Therefore, on account of the Jewish Day of Preparation and because the tomb was close by, they buried Jesus there.

---

[324] Exodus 12:46, Numbers 12:9; Psalm 34:20.
[325] Zechariah 12:10.
[326] Greek, *Ioudaios*.
[327] Around 6.5 gallons.
[328] Greek, *othonia*, see note 219.
[329] Greek, *tithemi*, and so in 19:42.

Chapter 20

20:1) On Sunday, the first day of the week, Mary Magdalene went to the tomb early in the morning. Even though it was still dark, she could see that the stone had been pushed away from the tomb. 20:2) Then she ran off and went to Simon Peter and the Other Disciple whom Jesus loved.[330] "Someone's taken the Lord from the tomb!" she exclaimed to them. "And we don't know where they've buried[331] him!"

20:3) Peter and the Other Disciple ran off at once and went to the tomb. 20:4) They were running together, but the Other Disciple was swifter, outdistanced Peter, and arrived first at the tomb. 20:5) The Other Disciple stooped down and peered inside. He saw the grave-linens arranged in a set place, but he did not go in just yet.

20:6) Then Simon Peter, who was following him, arrived. Peter entered the tomb and looked about at the grave-linens that were set to the side, 20:7) as well as the *soudarion*[332] that had covered Jesus' head. But the face-shroud was not in the same place as the grave-linens; rather, it had been folded up and was set apart

---

[330] John the Evangelist.
[331] Greek, *tithemi*, and so in 20:13 and 20:15.
[332] The face-shroud (cf. 11:44).

in a place by itself. 20:8) At that point, the Other Disciple, who had arrived first at the tomb, went inside. Then he beheld and believed. 20:9) (To that very moment, neither of them had understood the Scripture[333] that Jesus must rise from the dead.) 20:10) The two disciples departed and went back to their own homes.

20:11) However, Mary[334] remained standing, sobbing outside the tomb. As soon as[335] she wiped her tears, she stooped down and looked into the tomb. 20:12) She saw two angels in white garments sitting where the body of Jesus had been arranged, one where the head had been, the other at the feet.

20:13) "My Lady, why are you weeping?" the angels asked her.

"Because they took my Lord away," she replied to them, "and I do not know where they have buried him." 20:14) Just when she said this, she turned around[336] and beheld Jesus standing there, but she did not recognize him as Jesus.

---

[333] Psalm 16:10.

[334] Mary Magdalene, who had returned later that morning, as the sun was rising (cf. Matthew 28:1).

[335] See Appendix I.

[336] Greek, *estraphe eis ta opiso*. This expression is from Psalm 114 (113 LXX), which celebrates the triumph of the Exodus of Israel, the very image of the death and resurrection of Jesus, and the entry into the Promised Land. The phrase describes the moment when the River Jordan turned back on itself and the tribes of Israel crossed over into the Promised Land (Joshua 3). *Estraphe* appears

118

20:15) "My Lady," Jesus spoke to her, "why are you weeping? Whom do you seek?"

"Sir," she said to him, thinking he was the keeper of the garden, "if you are the one who moved him, tell me where you buried him, and I will take him."

20:16) "Mary," Jesus named her.

Falling backwards she cried out, "Rabbouni!" (meaning "Teacher"). [337]

20:17) "Touch me not," Jesus enjoined her, "for I am not yet ascended to Love. But go to my brothers and say to them, 'I ascend to my Father and to your Father, indeed to my Love and to your Love'!"

20:18) Mary Magdalene went and declared to the disciples that she had seen the Lord, and that he had said these things to her.

20:19) When it was evening on that very same day, Sunday – the first day of the week – the disciples were gathered together in one place, with the doors fastened shut because they were afraid of

---

again in 20:16 describing Mary Magdelene "falling backwards" at the recognition of Jesus, risen from the dead.
[337] Rabbouni is literally, "my great master."

the authorities.[338] Even though the doors were sealed shut, Jesus came and stood in their midst.

Jesus said to them, "Peace be with you," 20:20) After he said this he showed them his hands and his side. When they saw the Lord, the disciples rejoiced. 20:21) "Peace be with you," Jesus addressed them again. "Just as Love sent me, even so I send you." 20:22) After saying this, Jesus breathed on them and said, "Receive the Holy Spirit. 20:23) If you release someone's failings, they are released for them. If you hold fast their failings, held fast they remain."

20:24) But Thomas, one of the Twelve (the one called the "Twin"), was not with them when Jesus came. 20:25) The other disciples told him, "We have seen the Lord!"

But Thomas replied to them, "Unless I see in his hands the mark of the nails, and unless I put my finger into the wound of the nails, and I unless I stick my hand into his side, I will never believe!"

20:26) After eight days,[339] the disciples were again assembled inside, and Thomas was with them. Though the doors

---

[338] Greek, *Ioudaios.*
[339] The next Sunday, counting the Sunday of the Resurrection.

120

were sealed shut, Jesus came and stood in their midst. "Peace be with you," he proclaimed. 20:27) Then Jesus addressed Thomas, "Bring your finger here and probe my hands. And take your hand and put it into my side. Doubt no more. Believe!"

20:28) Thomas cried out to him, "O my Lord and my Love!"

20:29) "Because you have seen me, is it only now you believe?" Jesus said to him. "Happy and blessed are those who have seen nothing, and still they believe!"

20:30) Now the fact is that Jesus did many other signs in the presence of his followers that are not recorded. 20:31) These signs are written down so that you will believe that Jesus is the Christ, the Son of Love, and that with this faith, you will possess life by his name.

Chapter 21

21:1) Later on, Jesus manifested himself again to his disciples, this time by the Sea of Tiberias. This is how he appeared. 21:2) Simon Peter, Thomas (the one called the "Twin"), Nathaniel (who was from Cana of Galilee), the sons of Zebedee,[340] and two other of his disciples were all together.

21:3) "I'm going fishing," Simon Peter said to them.

"And we're coming with you." they replied.

Then they went off and set sail in their boat, but for all their efforts through the night, they caught not a thing. 21:4) As morning was breaking, Jesus was standing on the shoreline, but the disciples had no idea that it was Jesus.

21:5) "Little children!" Jesus called out to them, "have you caught anything to eat?"[341]

"No!" they shouted back.

21:6) "Cast the net out over the right side of the boat." Jesus directed them. "There's your find!"

---

[340] The Evangelist himself and his older brother, Iakovos (the Hellenized form of the Hebrew name Jacob, commonly rendered "James" in English).

[341] The "anything to eat" in Greek is a single word, *prosphagion*. The word means something eaten with bread, a eucharistic association that is borne out in verse 13. It can also mean fish in this context.

They cast the net out, but were unable to draw it up because of the size of the catch. 21:7) "It's the Lord!" the disciple, the one whom Jesus dearly loved,[342] exclaimed to Peter. When Simon Peter heard "It's the Lord," he tied his robe around his waist (he was to that moment bare-chested) and threw himself headlong into the sea.[343] 21:8) Then the other disciples came with the boat, dragging along the net with the fishes. They were not that far from shore, about 200 cubits.[344] 21:9) As soon as[345] they landed on the shore, they saw a carefully arranged bed of hot embers, a fish set over the coals, and some bread.

21:10) "Bring some of the fish that you caught just now," Jesus said to them.

21:11) Simon Peter went back and hauled the net up on dry land; it was bulging full of huge fishes – one hundred and fifty and three. And even though there were so many, the net did not tear.[346]

21:12) "Come," Jesus said to them, "eat some breakfast."

None of the disciples dared ask him, "Who are you?" for they knew it was the Lord. 21:13) Then Jesus got up and took the

---

[342] John the Evangelist.
[343] A joyous contrast to Luke 5:8, as well as to Matthew 14:28-30.
[344] A little over 100 yards.
[345] See Appendix I.
[346] Another contrast to Luke 5:6.

bread and gave it to them, and the fish likewise. 21:14) This was the third instance that Jesus showed himself risen from the dead to his disciples.

21:15) When they had finished eating, Jesus addressed Simon Peter, "Simon, son of Jonas, do you love[347] me more than these?"

"Yes, Lord," Peter said to him, "you know we are friends."[348]

Jesus said to him, "Nourish my little lambs." 21:16) A second time Jesus asked him again, "Simon, son of Jonas, do you love[349] me?"

"Yes, Lord, you know we are friends,"[350] Peter answered him.

"Shepherd my sheep." Jesus said to him. 21:17) A third time Jesus addressed him, "Simon, son of Jonas, are you my

---

[347] Greek, *agapao*.

[348] This expression translates the Greek, *Su oidas oti philo se*. This is usually translated by something akin to "You know that I love you." However, Jesus is asking for *agape*, a higher form of love; in verses 15 and 16 he asks "*agapas me?*" By translating *Su oidas oti philo se*, "You know we are friends," we highlight the distinction of the verbs used by Christ and by Peter, a distinction that is obvious in the original Greek. Christ asks for *agape* (sacrificial love) and Peter offers *philia* (friendship).

[349] Greek, *agapao*.

[350] Greek, *phileo*.

friend?"[351] Peter was downcast because Jesus had said, "are you my friend?" to him a third time.

"Lord," he insisted to Jesus, "you know everything! You know that I am your friend!"

"Pasture my sheep," Jesus said to him. 21:18) "Amen, amen, I say to you, when you were a young man, you girt yourself and walked wherever you pleased. But when you are old, you will stretch out your hands, and someone else will gird you, and force you on where you desire not." 21:19) (He said this to signify by what death Peter would glorify Love.)[352] After this pronouncement Jesus said to him, "Follow me."

21:20) Peter turned around and saw the disciple whom Jesus loved following behind, (the one who while reclining at the supper had leaned back on the chest of Jesus and asked, 'Lord, who is the one who betrays you?').[353]

21:21) Looking at that disciple, Peter asked Jesus, "Lord, what about him?"

---

[351] In this third questioning, Jesus changes the verb from *agapao* to *phileo*, accepting what Peter can offer. As Peter seems unaware of the implications of this exchange, he seems equally unaware that Jesus has just healed him of his three-fold denial (18:17 – 27).

[352] See footnote 242.

[353] John the Evangelist, cf. 13:25.

21:22) Jesus answered, "If I desire him to remain until I come, what is that to you? You, follow me."

21:23) Then a story[354] went out among the brethren, that this particular disciple was not going to die; but Jesus did not say to Peter that the disciple would not die, but rather, "If I desire him to remain until I come, what is that to you?"

21:24) This is the very disciple who bears witness about these things and has written these things. (And we[355] know that his witness is true). 21:25) There are so many other things that Jesus did. I suppose that if each and every one were to be recounted, the whole world could not contain the books that would have to be written.

Amen!

---

[354] Greek, *logos*.
[355] The hand of another, perhaps an amanuensis, is present here.

Appendix I

Did John Know Homer?
A Note on the Expression ὡς οὖν

When working with ancient Greek, every translator is confronted with the vexing problem of translating sentence adverbs, or particles. As Herbert Weir Smyth puts it, in the gold standard of Greek grammars: "To catch the subtle and elusive meaning of these often apparently insignificant elements of speech challenges the utmost vigilance and skill of the student."[356] During the translation of the present text, much consternation was created for the translators by the expression ὡς οὖν (*os oun*), a combination of a proclitic adverb and a postpositive particle.

Most English-language versions of the Gospel of John tend to translate this expression as a simple temporal transition, such as "when," "so when," or "therefore when."[357] The present translators struggled with this conventional treatment of *os oun*, whether it was sufficient to convey the inference of the Evangelist. Had John meant only "when," he might have used a number of other Greek transitional words or expressions, e.g., *ote* ("then"), which occurs eleven times in the Gospel of John. It seemed to us that the Evangelist might have chosen *os oun* with a specific intention.

---

[356] Herbert Weir Smyth, *op.cit.,* pg. 631, par. 2771.
[357] Rudolf Bultmann mentions three of these occurrences in his grammatical comments, 18:6, 20:11, and 21:9, citing all of them as parts of simple temporal sentences, *op. cit.*, pp. 635, 700.

Taking Smyth's maxim as a starting point, we embarked on a search for an alternate English translation and a deeper meaning of John's usage. A quick search revealed that in the entirety of Sacred Scripture (LXX and NT), the expression *os oun* occurs only eight times. The one Old Testament (LXX) usage in Esther 1:17, and the only non-Johannine New Testament usage, in Colossians 2:6, are non-temporal transitions. The other six occurrences are in the Gospel of John. This frequency alone is enough to merit our attention. These six instances of *os oun* are given below, underscored:

> 4:1) As soon as the Lord learned that the Pharisees had received reports saying, "Jesus is making and baptizing more disciples than John" –
> 4:40) As soon as the Samaritans reached Jesus, they asked him to remain with them.
> 11:6) But when Jesus heard that Lazaros was ill, he remained exactly where he was for two more days.
> 18:6) As soon as Jesus answered them, "I Am," they were all thrust backwards and fell to the ground.
> 20:11) However, Mary remained standing, sobbing outside the tomb. As soon as she wiped her tears, she stooped down and looked into the tomb.
> 21:9) As soon as they landed on the shore, they saw a carefully arranged bed of hot embers, a fish set over the coals, and some bread.

Checking with the authoritative handbook on Greek particles by J. D. Denniston, we discovered that the expression *os oun* has a distinct usage in Homer, occurring "with a verb of seeing, hearing or ascertaining.... In every case the object of the verb of seeing, etc., has been mentioned not long before."[358] The contexts of each instance in the Gospel of John either meet or suggest these criteria. Moreover, to our surprise, the last three of the six Johannine usages (18:6, 20:11, 21:9) occur in contexts evocative of Homeric counterparts. They are given below, with the Homeric citation first, followed by the Gospel.

Iliad, Γ 30 uses *os oun* in a description of Paris buckling at his sighting of Menelaus. The first excerpt, Γ 30-37, is given below from the Fagles translation (Book 3, lines 34-41),[359] with the translation of *os oun* in bold and underlined (as it will be in the next two examples).

> **But soon as** magnificent Paris marked Atrides
> shining among the champions, Paris' spirit shook.
> Backing into his friendly rank, he cringed from death
> as one who trips on a snake in a hilltop hollow
> recoils, suddenly, trembling grips his knees
> and pallor takes his cheeks and back he shrinks.
> So he dissolved again in the proud Trojan lines,
> dreading Atrides – magnificent, brave Paris.

This first parallel in the Gospel is part of the Passion narrative, the Betrayal. In John 18:6, at the moment Jesus is identified (he invokes the Divine "I Am"), Judas Iscariot and the soldiers collapse at his utterance.

> *18:1) When Jesus finished speaking, he moved on with his disciples to the other side of the Kidron Wadi, where there was a garden. Jesus entered the garden with his disciples. 18:2) Judas, who betrayed him, was familiar with the*

---

[358] J.D. Denniston, *The Greek Particles* (Oxford University Press, 1950), p. 417.
[359] Robert Fagles, *Homer The Iliad* (Viking, 1990), p. 129.

place, because Jesus would often gather there with his disciples. 18:3) Judas massed a company of garrison soldiers and some of the subordinates of the Chief Priests and Pharisees, and went there with torches, lanterns, and weapons.

18:4) Jesus, because he knew everything that was to come upon him, stepped forward and said, "Whom do you seek?"

18:5) "Jesus the Nazarene!" they shouted back at him.

"I Am," Jesus told them.

(Judas, the one who betrayed him, was standing right by the soldiers.)

*18:6) **As soon as** Jesus answered them, "I Am," they were all thrust backwards and fell to the ground.*

Odyssey, ω 391 uses *os oun* in the story of the recognition of Odysseus by his servant Dolius and Dolius' sons, and their being overcome by the experience. The passage ω 391-392 is given below, again in the Fagles translation (Book 24, lines 434-435).[360]

> **When** they saw Odysseus – knew him in their bones –
> they stopped in their tracks, staring, struck dumb,

In the second parallel, John 20:11, the scene is the encounter of Mary Magdalene and the risen Jesus (20:11-16), where Mary Magdalene nearly collapses as she recognizes Jesus.[361]

*20:11) However, Mary remained standing, sobbing outside the tomb. **As soon as** she wiped her tears, she stooped down and looked into the tomb. 20:12) She saw two angels*

---

[360] Robert Fagles, *Homer The Odyssey* (New York, Viking, 1996), p. 480.
[361] See footnote 336.

in white garments sitting where the body of Jesus had been arranged, one where the head would have been, the other at the feet.

20:13) "My Lady," why are you weeping?" the angels asked her.

"Because they took my Lord away," she replied to them, "and I do not know where they have buried him." 20:14) Just when she said this, she turned around and beheld Jesus standing there, but she did not recognize him as Jesus.

20:15) "My Lady," Jesus spoke to her, "why are you weeping? Whom do you seek?"

"Sir," she said to him, thinking he was the keeper of the garden, "if you are the one who moved him, tell me where you buried him, and I will take him.

20:16) "Mary," Jesus named her.

Falling backwards she cried out, "Rabbouni!" (meaning "Teacher").

In the *Odyssey*, γ 34, we hear *os oun* in the story of Telemachus' landing at Pylos and the reception and meal offered to him by King Nestor. The passage γ 34-40 is given below, (Book 3, lines 38-44):[362]

> **As soon as** they saw the strangers, all came crowding down,
> waving them on in welcome, urging them to sit.
> Nestor's son Pisistratus, first to reach them,
> grasped their hands and sat them down at the feast
> on fleecy throws spread out along the sandbanks,
> flanking his brother Thrasymedes and his father.
> He gave them a share of innards, poured some wine

---

[362] *Ibid*, p. 108.

In this final example, John 21:9, the scene is the mysterious Meal by the Sea of Galilee after the miraculous draught of fishes, following the Resurrection (21: 9-12).

> *21:9)* **_As soon as_** *they landed on the shore, they saw a carefully arranged bed of hot embers, and a fish set over the coals, and some bread.*
> *21:10) "Bring some of the fish that you caught just now," Jesus said to them.*
> *21:11) Simon Peter went back and hauled the net up on dry land; it was bulging full of huge fishes – one hundred and fifty and three. And even though there were so many, the net did not tear.*
> *21:12) "Come," Jesus said to them, "eat some breakfast." None of the disciples dared ask him, 'Who are you?' for they knew it was the Lord.*

These examples pose fascinating questions. Was the Evangelist John consciously evoking the poetic trope of Homer's use of *os oun*? Did this trope evoke for his intended audience the same sudden realized physical presence of one who had heretofore been unrecognized? Of course, there is no way of saying for certain, but the fact remains that each of these occurrences of *os oun* is clearly best translated with this Homeric usage and its dramatic implications, and these occurrences are found uniquely in this Gospel.

Appendix II

A Note on the Word *Ioudaios*

Of the 86 times that the word *Ioudaios* (Greek, Ἰουδαῖος, pl. *Ioudaioi,* Ἰουδαῖοι) occurs in the Gospels, 70 of these instances occur in the Gospel of John (in the Textus Criticus, 71). Most known translations (e.g., KJV, RSV, NASB, NIV) translate the term using "Jew(s)," or "Jewish," in the case of a clear adjectival usage. This blanket analogue approach, together with hypotheses seeking to explain the frequency of the word in John, have created a theology of blame that is both irresponsible and harmful to the relationship between Christians and Jews.

It is not our purpose here to examine why anti-Semitism has so stained the history of the Christian Faith. Rather, we wish to provide both an accurate and corrective vision for the translation of *Ioudaios* in the Gospel of John that lends itself to addressing Christian anti-Semitism. Thus, we are committed to translating the word *Ioudaios* consistent with its meaning within the text. (A listing by verse is at the end of this appendix.)

The translators feel very strongly that the Gospel of John itself does not contain any anti-Semitism. However, we would readily acknowledge that translators and commentators alike have followed the path blazed by Rudolf Bultmann, the most influential Biblical scholar of the twentieth century, whose analysis of the term has had a lasting and deleterious effect on subsequent scholarship. To wit:

"The term *oi Ioudaioi*, characteristic of the Evangelist, gives an overall portrayal of the Jews, viewed from the standpoint of Christian faith, as the representatives of unbelief (and thereby, as will appear, of the unbelieving "world" in general). The Jews are spoken of as an alien people, not merely from the point of view of the Greek readers, but also, and indeed only properly, from the stand-point of faith; for Jesus himself speaks to them as a stranger and correspondingly, those in whom the stirrings of faith or of the search for Jesus are to be found are distinguished from the "Jews", even if they are themselves Jews. ... *This usage leads to the recession or to the complete disappearance of the distinctions made in the Synoptics between different elements in the Jewish people.*"[363]

This line of argument has been accepted, in one form or another, by virtually every succeeding generation of modern scholars. On a psychological level, it interprets the motivations of the Evangelist. On a linguistic level, it completely disallows any use of synecdoche, the linguistic device that uses a part for the whole, as in "sail" to mean "ship," or, most importantly in this case, *a whole for the part*. As we shall see below, synecdoche simply and easily accounts for this "complete disappearance of

---

[363] Rudolf Bultmann, *op. cit.*, pg. 86, (emphasis added).

the distinctions made in the Synoptics between different elements in the Jewish people."[364]

Elaine Pagels of Princeton University follows the lead of Bultmann in her book, *The Origin of Satan*, when she states the following: "Anyone who reads the gospel of John can see that 'the Jews' have become for John what Bultmann sees as a symbol of human evil."[365] She dismisses Bultmann's 'symbolizing' as an "apologetic evasion,"[366] and ascribes to the Evangelist an active anti-Semitic intention:

> "John's decision to make an actual, identifiable group – among Jesus' contemporaries and his own – into a symbol of "all evil" obviously bears religious, social, and political implications. ... Having cast "the Jews" in that role, John's gospel can arouse and even legitimate hostility towards Judaism...."[367]

What is most disturbing about this line of reasoning is that it has become ensconced within academic circles, as witnessed by the following quote from James Carroll's monumental work, *Constantine's Sword, The Church and the Jews, A History*. Here is his reference to the previous work of Pagels:

> "Pagels shows how, with the last Gospel, John, dating to around 100 and clearly reflecting the

---

[364] Ibid.

[365] Elaine Pagels, *The Origin of Satan* (Random House, Inc., 1995), pp. 103, 104.

[366] *Ibid.*

[367] *Op. cit.*, p.105.

intensification of intra-Jewish sectarian conflict that followed the destruction of the Temple, *the identification of "the Jews" and Satan himself has become complete.* This movement is reflected in the fact that the loaded phrase "the Jews" (in Greek, *hoi Ioudaioi*) appears a total of 16 times in the Gospels of Mark, Matthew and Luke, while in John it appears 71 *[sic]* times. As Pagels says, "John chooses to tell the story of Jesus as a story of cosmic conflict – conflict between divine light and primordial darkness, between the close-knit group of Jesus' followers and the implacable, sinful opposition they encountered from the 'world'." But in John Jesus himself identifies the evil one with the people. The "temptation scenes," which are played out in other Gospels between Jesus and Satan, are played out in John between Jesus and the people. *This is why the phrase "the Jews" appears so frequently."* [368]

The present translators disagree wholeheartedly with these analyses, especially identifying the Jewish people with Satan! Not only do they make an anti-Jewish polemic intrinsic to the text, something that even Bultmann saw only as symbolic, but they also ignore understanding the text within its own context, straining to arrive at a logic to explain the frequency of the word, *Ioudaios*. A

---

[368] James Carroll, *Constantine's Sword, The Church and the Jews, A History* (Houghton Mifflin Company, 2001), p. 92, (emphasis added).

clear example of why contextual translation is necessary –
especially from a perspective of logic, is the following passage:

> 11:54) Consequently, Jesus no longer walked
> openly among the *Ioudaioi*. Rather, he withdrew
> from there to an area close to the desert, to a town
> called Ephraim. There, Jesus passed the time with
> his disciples.

If "*Ioudaioi*" were to be translated "Jews," the passage
would make no sense. Jesus, in going to Ephraim, is still in the
company of "Jews," as he was continually when in the presence of
his disciples, all of whom were Jews, even as he was. Rather,
"*Ioudaioi*" should be translated as "Judeans," the very group of
people whom Jesus would have avoided by withdrawing "from
there," the environs of Jerusalem, to Ephraim in the first place.
Translating *Ioudaios* as Judean(s) is a common sense approach,
particularly in chapters 11 and 12, where the locality of Jerusalem
calls for this distinction. Remember that Jesus and most of his
followers were Galileans, who though Jews by religion, were
considered different enough from Judeans (their fellow Jewish
brethren), that even their accent was identifiable (cf. Matthew
26:73).

The same logic applies for the next two passages, where
clearly, it is the *authorities* that are feared; whether that be the
Sanhedrin, the Temple constabulary, or the sectarian leadership,
not their co-religionists:

138

> 19:38) Later on, Joseph of Arimathaia (a follower of Jesus – although a secret one, because he was afraid of the *Ioudaioi*) begged Pilate that he might retrieve the Body of Jesus,

and,

> 20:19) When it was evening on that very same day, Sunday – the first day of the week – the disciples were gathered together in one place, with the doors fastened shut because they were afraid of the *Ioudaioi*.

In the view of the present translators, the point of view held by many in the modern academic community grossly misrepresents the Gospel, and actually contributes to the nagging anti-Semitism in Christianity that they work so rightly to undo. The effect of an unthinking blanket translation of the word *Ioudaios* undervalues the nuance demanded by the context. Unfortunately, the consequences for the relations between Jews and Christians have been devastating and are in need of much healing.

Words count. Christians have a responsibility to speak in ways that foster the purpose of the Gospel and not distort the sense of Scripture. We believe that by using synecdoche (whole for part) and translating "sense for sense" and not slavishly "word for word" (as St. Jerome so wisely advises[369]), the meaning of the Evangelist is more fairly and more accurately represented.

---

[369] St. Jerome, Letter 57 (to Pammachius): *non verbum e verbo sed sensum de sensu.*

Below, we list the seventy instances in the Gospel of John where the word *Ioudaios* is used (most have a footnote), so that readers may compare for themselves and see the logic of translating text within context.

John 1:19	religious authorities
John 2:6	Jewish
John 2:13	Jewish
John 2:18	Judeans
John 2:20	they
John 3:1	Judeans
John 3:25	certain Judean
John 4:9	Jew
John 4:9	Jews
John 4:22	we Jews
John 5:1	Jewish
John 5:10	some people
John 5:15	the people
John 5:16	religious authorities
John 5:18	religious authorities
John 6:4	Jewish
John 6:41	some of the people
John 6:52	they
John 7:1	religious authorities
John 7:2	Jewish
John 7:11	Judeans
John 7:13	religious authorities
John 7:15	Some of the people
John 7:35	people
John 8:22	some people
John 8:31	the people
John 8:48	they
John 8:52	they
John 8:57	they
John 9:18	The authorities

John 9:22	the religious authorities
John 9:22	the authorities
John 10:19	the local people
John 10:24	a group
John 10:31	some of the people
John 10:33	they
John 11:8	Judeans
John 11:19	its inhabitants
John 11:31	Judeans
John 11:33	the Judeans
John 11:36	people
John 11:45	Judeans
John 11:54	Judeans
John 11:55	Jewish
John 12:9	Judeans
John 12:11	Judeans
John 13:33	Judeans
John 18:12	the religious authorities
John 18:14	the leadership
John 18:20	believers
John 18:31	they
John 18:33	Jews
John 18:35	Jew
John 18:36	them
John 18:38	the crowd
John 18:39	Jews
John 19:3	Jews
John 19:7	the leaders
John 19:12	the leadership
John 19:14	the crowd
John 19:19	Jews
John 19:20	people
John 19:21	omitted as redundant
John 19:21	Jews
John 19:21	Jews

John 19:31	religious authorities
John 19:38	religious authorities
John 19:40	Jewish
John 19:42	Jewish
John 20:19	authorities

Acknowledgments

Thanking all those who have shared with me their insights and knowledge would be impossible; therefore, I shall not make such a futile attempt. Rather, I would like to recognize the contribution of three persons, without whom, I would not have brought this work to completion.

First, my wife, Lyn, whose constant encouragement and diligent work created the look and feel of this book. Second, Patra Sevastiades, whose keen editorial eye brought much-needed suggestions of clarity to the whole of the work. Third, Dr. Anthony Bossis, who has been more than a friend to me and to this book. All three of them embody *sophia*, the wisdom that brings meaning, and they have inspired me to seek after it.

For any errors I take full responsibility, hoping that thanks to the hard work and support of others, they are as few as possible.

Made in the USA
Middletown, DE
13 February 2017